T0196477

BRING BACK
THE LATE 90s
AND EARLY
2000s

THE NOSTALGIA MANIFESTO

TRAVIS SMITH

BALBOA.
PRESS

A DIVISION OF HAY HOUSE

Balboa Press books may be ordered through booksellers or by contacting:

Balboa Press
A Division of Hay House
1663 Liberty Drive
Bloomington, IN 47403
www.balboapress.com.au
1 (877) 407-4847

Because of the dynamic nature of the Internet, any web addresses or links contained in this book may have changed since publication and may no longer be valid. The views expressed in this work are solely those of the author and do not necessarily reflect the views of the publisher, and the publisher hereby disclaims any responsibility for them.

The author of this book does not dispense medical advice or prescribe the use of any technique as a form of treatment for physical, emotional, or medical problems without the advice of a physician, either directly or indirectly. The intent of the author is only to offer information of a general nature to help you in your quest for emotional and spiritual well-being. In the event you use any of the information in this book for yourself, which is your constitutional right, the author and the publisher assume no responsibility for your actions.

Any people depicted in stock imagery provided by Getty Images are models, and such images are being used for illustrative purposes only. Certain stock imagery © Getty Images.

Print information available on the last page.

ISBN: 978-1-5043-1345-2 (sc)
ISBN: 978-1-5043-1344-5 (e)

Balboa Press rev. date: 06/14/2018

CHAPTER 1

Modern Day Tragedy

"The iPhone is always on," said Davies. "always in the background, always more important than getting off your backside and getting to work for many young people.

"The latest batch of young people lack any drive or desire to work – largely thanks to the warm, punch-drunk, sedated feeling of being permanently online to their friends on the internet."

That's an article from the International Business Times by Tom Porter. I read that before writing this introduction, so you have an introduction as to what I'm trying to display here. Humanity has become overly dependent and narcotized on technology... smart phones and touch screen technology. These objects pacify a human mind; they juice a person into a mindless drone absorbed in a bubble wrap of desensitized fiction. Humans are on a stairwell towards a jelly fish existence.......where people don't have to think with their brains but with a control system telling them what to click, watch, listen to and follow. It doesn't matter what age they are. I see it every day. You'd rather be on a Samsung, or on a Facebook that you can't smell, taste or walk into. Billions are in this digital nonexistent cage, one with no walls or boundaries like the Matrix where everyone is interconnected. How people everywhere are plugged into the same virtual interface is a global horror.

The human race has now become apathetic, lazy and more over indulgent when they're given power at the touch of a screen, to a point where you wouldn't raise your head to see the stars come out at night, but instead text someone in the next room about what they're eating; pre-occupied with trivia and mindless garbage, giving a lethargic downplaying to everything else in life. Where women have no jubilation for their new born.... instead reporting what they went through on a Facebook status, trivializing an important and sacred passage in human life to nothing more than a promotional day at the office. It's pure and unapologetic vanity that has consumed modern society.

Kids become desensitized as they're brought up in this sponge, until humanity's dependence has given birth to nothing more than ruin. I mean I never believed we would be walking around with smart phones attached to our irises every waking minute of the day. Can you fathom what everyone has turned into? A robotic drone walking the streets of civilization with no thought or concern for reality, no concept of the world we're living in, and no intention of moving forward by acknowledging the world around us. It's suitable enough to never change for everyone because smart phones are a sedating pacifier. We're as good as dead if we pacify ourselves and stay glued to its gaze for an eternity.

I want to wake up from this virtual hallucination of Hell and fall onto a bedroom carpet in the year 1999, when everything was simpler, when technology didn't saturate our diaries of something personal and close.

Today we have no personal sincerity now that we've given everything away to technology...our secrets, our livelihoods, our favourite foods and what our opinions think on everything that's personal to us. We have no honest self. Facebook has stolen what it means to be human....to have a special place in your heart for something no one else could ever understand or cuddle you for. That's what this book is about, a diary of my thoughts and deep seated feelings. We've become a numb species of robots addicted to Facebook and Twitter.

This manifesto begins with the present day but it goes back to the late 90s and early 2000s, the best musical entertainment and pop culture young people ever experienced. There was food, there was sun, and Spring Break came as you are like Nirvana. The seasons changed but we were always close and never resorted to feverish displays of online introverted existence. We were outside doing things and being the life of the party back then, the times when we could look at the stars and appreciate being juvenile in youth, where you could walk the beach at 5 am and listen to Yellow by Coldplay as the sun perched its morning gaze over the horizon. When there was fervour for longing and expression, there was no such thing as egotistical glorification like men and women in today's music industry. It wasn't about you, it was about what you could create with your heart and soul and immersion.

The turn of the millennium had American Pie 2, where chicks had an aroma of coolness to them, you remember those days? Well lucky for you, because I was only 6 during the turn of the century. I wouldn't remember those glory days like you and your friends felt in your teenage years, but I sure as hell can depict what it must have tickled like, the nostalgia that must taste like whipped cream warm with cinnamon donuts and jam in your mouth. Songs like Teenage Dirt bag by Wheatus, in that thick American vernacular with a crystal clear spoken 'R' in every syllable that made USA accents sound so gullible and college innocent, if you can remember its growing up lyrics –

"Herr name is Noelle, I have a dream about her she rings my bells, I got gym class in half an hour and oh how she rrrocks.....In Keds and tube socks...but she doesn't know who I am'

I wish those days would return and last an eternity. Americans got double lucky with nostalgia and pronunciation. So why can't we go back there and defy the future? Why don't the radio stations play those songs and girls still talk to each other rather than stare into their smart phones? Where's the innocence and vitality of youth where nothing else mattered but ourselves and not the smart phone or a Facebook status? But instead of keds and tube socks, what we're left with is today's illusion is a fabricated sense of identity.

It comes as the final nail in the coffin to a society functioning on a dork's internet memes and childish smart phone apps. Today there is an incoherent and poorly thought out music trend; Hip Hop has lost its iconic baggy clothes and street culture, now turning rappers into tight jean wearing, mumbling morons. Modern Hip Hop is a joke; it's a pretentious egotistical display of women, jewellery and sports cars with idiots who look feminine and cowardly. At least Tupac wore trousers that were sloppy and confrontational and had rhymes that spoke of struggle and hardship. Music has gone down the gurgler, dub step, hardstyle, mumble rap, auto tuned synthesizers, they're all plasticity with no emotional brilliance. It's a last cry from a dying Humanity trying to claw out of an ocean of gluttony and laziness to intelligently craft anything ourselves. A recycling of the worst garbage from the 80s with digitally advanced spin to their sounds, it's all been perverted into a cyber melody, which is impossible to connect to, because humans have no discreet belonging to a computer way of thinking. Dub Step and Hardstyle have no emotional fortitude to make you think about things the way a piano does, or a flute would if it went right with a guitar and the singer knew how to compensate your emotional tenderness between thoughts and memories, the amount of talent and fortitude it takes to play an instrument and make others think with your imagination is the reason why we can watch movies together and share the same feelings. If you could put your new born to sleep by carefully strumming next to their pillow and watch them dream about what you're creating.....then you really are sharing the feeling of music in a young mind. Like that song Mad World by Gary Jules, the lyrics are spot on –

'All around me are familiar faces, worn out places, worn out faces, bright and early for the daily races, going nowhere....going nowhere'

That song reminds me about the modern world of vanity. A mad world and I'm seeing more similarities in the songs of the past I listen to. Modern garbage you hear on the radio wouldn't understand how to make you feel grief, or loneliness, or desire, perhaps love or longing, fear or whatever it is that human sympathies display. It could never bring comfort to your ears like the fertility of a woman's voice breezing into your thoughts and reducing your stresses in a song like Don't Speak by Gwen Stefani –

'You and me......we use to be together.....every day together, always, I really feel like I'm losing my best friend, I can't believe this could be the end. It looks as though you're...letting go. And if it's real then I don't want to know'

Feel the tenderness of Don't Speak. The song is a classic, from a time when music was intimate and not lobotomized; Gwen perfected an illustration of human dignity and imagination just with her words that she spoke pure and genuine. There's no older sisters' cuddle in the processed auto tunes of today, there's no girlfriend with the scent of beach morning sand in her hair. The Under the Bridge parts of Red Hot Chille Peppers and the silk of nostalgia...that's what made music so good. It was your mind reminding you of the times when you hear good caresses in a song with strings, chords or tunes with a voice and soul. I'm bringing this point of view to you if you can unplug for a second.

It's like everywhere I look people are absorbed, they're consumed absolutely in the drivel of their smart phone, everywhere, on every street corner, every bus stop, every train station, when you walk into a cafe, a super market, a fast food outlet, a restaurant, even in their own homes. It's visual and psychological slavery; it's mankind's mind that's been stolen by passive acquiescence. This is what apathy and abstract materialism breed in the West; it's what makes self loving women take selfies caked up in makeup because they want to be worshipped. It's what makes people lavish in hollow depictions of narcissistic indulgence. Its self adulation gone mad, the world is falling all around us and you're not even noticing it.

Despite all that, there was once a time when everything was mango flavoured with a residue peeling of bliss. Cause that's all we have left, archives of memories. The late 90s and early 2000s were a time and place like no other, specifically from 1998 – 2003. Some would disagree and say the 60s were better, or the 70s but you have to allow me to explain why the turn of the millennium was the coolest. So where do we begin? Well let's start with some famous lyrics and see if you remember –

'The heart is a bloom...shoots up through the stony ground.... there's no room. No space to rent in this town. You're out of luck. And the reason that you had to care...the traffic is stuck. And you're not moving anywhere'

Beautiful Day by U2 is a song that imbues any listener with a sense of affection and joy. After hearing that you'll see why that time period was the greatest yearbook ever, how it's warm fluorescent comfort when lovers kiss or when Bono eats an apple melts into your reservoirs of nostalgia. No, seriously, watch it on You Tube and see why this book is dedicated to those times.

Beautiful Day U2

There were multitudes of other songs, all with that same vibe and nostalgia from bands like Greenday to Blink 182 and The Offspring. I know there are plenty of you out there who were young at the time and agree today that it should come back. But like that Offspring song.....it seems to have Gone Away. I take great love for the time, even the clothing for people who were young and rebellious. Why would clothing matter? Everybody wears clothes and it's their choice what they wear. But here's my problem, when concerning fashion for both sexes in their youth, and especially in the 90s this idea was applied…. confrontation was synonymous with how baggy your clothes were. Let me further explain this concept; baggy trousers and the criminal image is what made American youth culture cool, while today, too many young men are proud of their chinos hugging their legs and having tight pants. Tight slim fits make a dude look meek and timid; tights give the impression of being a wimp that's got no backbone. They wear slim fits as a sign they're afraid of the alpha male in baggy Nike trousers with dragon tats up his neck and arms, pumping iron and dreaming about his next brawl. People who wear skinny chinos are usually college types who listen to Ed Sheeran or Taylor Swift….while bros and alpha girls listen to Bullet with a name by Nonpoint or Room to Breathe by Project Wyze. Give them a try and see if you can handle testosterone in music. The latter two songs will inject your blood with so much testosterone you'd eat bricks and piss napalm. Bullet with a Name and Room to Breathe would be vilified today because of over dosage of manhood and Rottweiler aggression in their content.

And now look at today's music….it's because skinny jeans have pussified men. Think about it, tight tailor-made pants on a guy, which only serves to give off an effeminate appearance. Young boys who should be scrapping with each other in fist fights or chasing chicks with an air of chauvinism now have twitter in their eyes all day, being social butterflies while wearing the tightest most effeminate clothing imaginable. Teenagers today live and dwell on their smart phones and social media accounts. They fight and bitch about each other behind their backs through the power of scrolling, checking their feeds on their statuses and responding to petty challenges with words and jargon. You can't make warriors out of that type of silky material. Today is a pathetic generation. If there's one thing I've come to see about the world it is that people are products of their environment. Now lemme tell you about a different culture.

During the height of coast to coast war between Biggie Smalls and Tupac, American music was changing from Madonna and

Seattle Grunge into a tidal wave of carnivorous, street brawling, drunk-on-murder culture that was Hip Hop. No.... not the Hip Hop you're familiar with; not the mumbling, auto corrected, half educated, moronic clowns who look more piss weak and soft than fashion designers. I'm talking about a street culture that was put on the microphone, where blazing rival enemies with a Mac 10 and being soaked in their blood was an honour for these killers.

And so with this fusion of violence and animosity came the clothing style.... baggy jeans that were so loose and sloppy you could conceal an AK-47 in the front and a bazooka in the back of them things. Tall tee shirts that draped down around your knee caps, Christian necklaces and dog tags, this was some serious shit I'm talking. Ain't no online war on some twitter account, no mumbling behind a mic, you walked the streets of Brooklyn or Queensbridge with a Glock in one hand and your fingers crossed in the other. It's like Mobb Deep with Survival of the fittest –

'There's a war going on outside no man is safe from, you can run but you can't hide from these streets that we done took, you're walking with your head down scared to look, you shook, cause ain't no such things as half way crooks'

Seriously reader....for your own sake....get a glimpse of that mentality, go onto You Tube and watch if modern rappers would last against these dudes –

Shook Ones Part 2 by Mobb Deep

The 90s was a decade of gang culture, American hoodlums hit the big time with Ezy E, Biggie Smalls, Tupac, Nas, Rakim, Ice Cube, Big Pun and Big L, every one of those names mentioned represented the urban battlefields of American cities between rival homies. Street music was at its most lethally injected containing a substance of virulent attitude.

The same cultural relics of super baggy clothing, street wear, attitude and propensity to violence continued into the early 21st century. This was the age of Eminem, who further glorified the murder, the misogyny, the robberies and the aggression. Because it was during the 1990s, leading up to the 21st century that created Eminem, where men became men again; they rediscovered their sense of testosterone and masculinity from the disaster that was the 80s. You see the 1980s feminized males, it taught glam fashion and men to paint their finger nails. They had eye liner and lip stick while walking around in high heels on stage. That type of rubbish is anti-masculinity and anti-testosterone. Look at examples such as Kiss, Twisted Sister or even Prince. These individuals were girly and femalized, which should never occur in an animal as confrontational and obtuse as a male. The 80s trend of glam rock and long Buffy hair was a calamity to American pop culture society. That is until a saviour of the world came along called the 1990s.

You see people remember the 90s for Kurt Kobain and Nirvana, a Seattle grunge band that popularized flannel. I personally enjoy a lot of Nirvana's music, and I can appreciate the artistic depth and talent that Kobain possessed. He had more testosterone than most of them girly glam bands from the 80s. His music was hard; it was pissed off and talked about suffering and neglect. It was cynical; the 90s are remembered for its cynicism on life. But apart from Kobain there were other bands that rediscovered male hormones. I'll give you an example....ever heard of Rage against the Machine? Compare the name Rage against the Machine to Twisted Sister. That's proof that the 90s brought back aggressive testosterone in men and not weird androgynous shit. Think about it, listen to Killing in the Name, in that rebellious bark at the end –

'Fuck you I won't do what you tell me!'

Killing in the name was killing subtleties in people's brains in 1992...Rage against the Machine paved the way for more aggression, more anger, and more edginess for later bands. They were revolutionary. Then off course there's another band that amplified temperament in males during the outbreak of the 90s; that band was Pantera. Pantera's lead singer Phil Anselmo was hyped on masculinity, with a shaved head, tats and an aggressive appearance and it showed in his brutish voice, songs like No Good (Attack the Radical) and Walk brought more of this alpha male type back into the spotlight. It was this movement in the early 90s such as Rage against the Machine and Pantera that cemented the return of the alpha male. And that's where we come to our next point. A new breed of rock music was coming of age in the 90s. In its fledgling state this new and different type of rock would eventually take America and the world by storm.

The electric guitars used for this new rock style were not the screeching cords people were accustomed to, no, this new breed of guitars were tuned way down in a sludgy thud so that the sound was grumbling, deep and blunt like a car exhaust pipe. This next evolution of rock was called Nu Metal.

No one had heard Nu Metal before because it was something completely different. Up until 1994 the only rock bands that were hitting the big time were Nirvana and Pearl Jam along with a few others, their grunge sound was the buzz. But unknown to the world, a small Nu Metal band from Bakersfield, California, was emerging and gaining traction in the music world. This band was different in every way because they styled themselves on a sporty appearance. They wore Adidas tracksuits, baggy denim and tall tees. They had dreadlocks for hair. This new band was the creation of a new image, a new sound, a new breed of rock. This band....was Korn.

Korns debut album was like nothing, and I mean NOTHING rock had ever experienced before. Not even Rage or Pantera matched their sound. Fiedly's bass guitar was deep and tormenting, like beat boxing with the back of your throat. The two lead guitars were groovy while also evil and sickening; mixed with the bass guitar, this new sound produced a barking thump similar to an exhaust pipe if it went with a grizzlies shout.

Nu Metal became the pinnacle of testosterone, where young men in triple XL shirts and baggy denim, thick goatees and dreadlocks finally realized.... providence had selected them to conquer the world of pop culture. From now on men would never wear tights; they would never degrade their masculinity by smearing their faces with lip stick and eye shadow, no more finger nail painting, no more feminine features. Everything was centred on machismo, on confrontation, on antagonism. Korn centred their music on confrontation...with a song like Blind. Check it out, I ask you the reader to watch the following music video for educational purposes as to why testosterone is needed in men, take note of the baggy clothes and the most aggressive guitar sound of the 90s –

Blind by Korn

It starts off slow...but once that sludgy guitar kicks in, you're gonna cop an eargasm of the birth of Nu Metal

Within five years of Korn's debut self titled album, Nu Metal was the biggest thing on tha planet. It outshined Britney Spears and NSNYC as the biggest music culture in America. Other bands of the genre, who also tuned down their guitars and added hip hop lyrics and turn tables, became platinum selling acts. By the year 2000 boy bands were being overshadowed by this aggressive genre. And the biggest Nu Metal band of them all was one that encouraged the very personality that is embedded in a bro.

This band encouraged jocks to be top dogs, a band that really emphasises the word 'confrontation' with its front man. The band sold over a million units with their 3rd album in its opening week in October 2000, thanks to the lead singers' reputation for being confrontational. Many people don't like the singer because of his bro mentality, his persona to get in your face while pumped up on bravado. But most people are pussies and have never been in a fist fight, this guy copped a life full of shovelling shit and it moulded him into a hardcore, thick skinned, backward cap wearing cool motherfucker. Personality traits that are usually reserved for the MMA Octagon ring, he brought this tough guy mentality into the world of American youth and it became contagious, turning teenagers and young adults into rebellious bros and women into tomboys. For once it was cool to kick ass, it was cool to insinuate and be bad mouthed, sloppy looking and cold hearted. You probably know what band I'm talking about. If not, I'll give you an example –

'I pack a chainsaw, I'll skin your ass raw, and if my day keeps this way I just might....break your fucking face tonight'

If this song came out today the millennials would need a safe space because they were raised like fucking pussies. But teenagers in the late 90s were not pussies. Which is why they fought like Lions in Iraq and Afganistan, and I'll show you exactly why. Watch this next song and realize why this group made American bros and bad bitches the coolest attituders on Earth –

Break Stuff by Limp Bizkit

For those who like baggy clothes, girls with attitude and American brawler mentality then keep rollin' rollin' rollin wearing baggy denim with rebel babes dancing behind you in a song of the same name. That's My Generation.

Because the music of those early years cemented a certain type of attitude in its listeners, it brought out the mammal in your blood and you wanted to let loose. It doesn't matter if it was Hip Hop or rock, there was something in the air....the oxygen was contaminated with a hundred thousand milligrams of angst. When the Americans went to war immediately after 9/11 they didn't need permission to put a bullet through your brain, the edgy culture motivated a deep seated level of animosity.

I can't explain it but there was something in the air. A virile nihilism and coldness, and it showed up in Eminem's music or with

President Bush's willingness to attack Iraq and unleash American military might to bring forth 21st century Armageddon. It showed up in video games, too, where little kids had their tender minds fondled by war. When you mix badass lyrical content with displays of US secret intelligence activities around the world you get one game that illuminated the back alley way behaviour by a modern day assassin. You know what game I'm talking about? No....not Assassins Creed; that is a cool game in its own right. But this one I'm describing puts forward the existence of America's deadliest hunters. I'm talking....about the original Splinter Cell. Splinter Cell reflected the cultural amber of American fear in the early 21st century, the distrust of foreign governments outside inherent US interests. The game was something different.

But what's more, is an animated clip from the beginning of the game where Sam Fisher is in a transport plane over an ocean and is suiting up. He conceals his weapon, zips up his Velcro vest and attaches an ear piece. His immediate superior gives him a description of the situation.

"Nikolai just declared war on the US; the Georgians hit our communication, transportation, power grids we still don't know how extensive the damage is. Your mission just became critical'

Presented with the illest song of 2002, Name of the Game by Crystal Method. Maybe you haven't played Splinter Cell, maybe you're not interested, but I won't disappoint when I say Name of the Game by Crystal Method is fucking badass to the core.

CHAPTER 2

The Movies of The Millennium

Aside from music, Hollywood had a touch of picture quality you don't see today. You're probably unaware of the difference in quality between a movie from the millennium and a movie from today. But what I'm about to tell you makes a huge difference and will change your perception. Take a neo modern film like The Avengers or any super hero movie recently, regardless of the acting or the action what truly sticks in my mind with great annoyance is the look and feel of such modern movies. What could be so annoying about them apart from the shitty dialogue and cheesy action? One thing stands above all else in blasphemy....the digital camera. Over these last few years Hollywood has undergone a transition in the way films are recorded.

For most of Hollywood history ever since its beginning movies were always recorded on celluloid. Celluloid for those who don't know is those coil reels you see in a camera stock. But celluloid represented something more than just plastic strips; they personified the dominant format throughout Hollywood history – 35mm film. 35mm film, or any film for that matter including 70mm, had a graceful texture and grain to their look and appearance. There was a photo chemical beauty in the process of shooting film, and just ask Quentin Tarantino, Christopher Nolan or Steven Spielberg, Hollywood's greatest directors completely agree that film in its texture and grade is far more pleasing to watch than digital according to interviews in which they're lent their opinions on the subject. Now why does this matter?

Well it matters because if you have a rich visual taste, you can spot the difference between an acrylic painting and an oil painting. It's the same in movies. Digital movies lack the lurid and vibrant depth that film has. You probably don't care because you don't know the difference in either; you look at a movie and like a dummy you just watch it. But I guess a dummy can drink good liquor too and not notice the difference between Tennessee Whiskey and Scotch. It's people that don't know the difference that are the problem, but for those of you who do know the difference between Jack Daniels and Johnny Walker, for those of you who do know the difference between Osama Bin Laden and Saddam Hussein, for those of you who do know the difference between the US Army and the US Marines, please read the following and know the difference.... film is superior to digital. That shouldn't even be explained. But unfortunately Hollywood has fucked with good man's tastes in filmography, and it's pissing me off something severe. If there's one thing I like its taste in good things, I like Bourbon and coke, late 90s music and I enjoy 35 mm film for my visual dose of pleasure.

In fact everybody secretly desires 35mm film over digital even if they don't know it, you know it sub consciously. Want to know why? I'll tell you why...did you enjoy watching the movie The Dark Knight? The Dark Knight with Heath Ledger in his memorable performance as the Joker....terrific acting, superb set locations, brilliant suspense blah blah errrrr WRONG! Answer me this question in all sincerity....did you enjoy the look of the film? The red face paint that illuminated Joker's lips, the rich oranges in every explosion when a fire ball balloons, those tasty yellows when Bruce Wayne and Harvey Dent go to dinner with Rachel. Or how Batman sits atop a sky scraper and glides over the city with illicit blues and sensual greys at night? When I say a rich visual taste...I mean rich visual taste when your eyes watch something that ignites the deepest passions in us. Guess what format the Dark Knight was shot on....correct...35mm Film. Just do this one thing for me to clarify visuals.....do this one thing. Watch the trailers from the Dark Knight movies and pay keen attention to the hues and ambience of the colours –

The Dark Knight and Dark Knight Rises trailers

Both movies were shot on celluloid. Tell me I'm wrong when I say film is beautiful to look at because making movies is not about letting people watch something average, there has to be an artwork to it. Steven Spielberg didn't have a maddening passion as a child for film because he just wanted people to watch something ordinary; he had an artwork in his brain that needed motion and texture and sound and colour and he knew he could bring that art to life and breathe life into its lungs. An imagination and creative visual style by using something called a film camera, a tool that Pablo Picasso wished he had, Spielberg had that tool to harness the allure of his mind. It's not about the characters or their personalities; it's about the image you can create. Making movies is like being Vincent Van Gogh, making movies is recording visual images in a way that displays your imagination, your dreams, everything you could ever think of, it could be about ghosts; it could be dinosaurs, ancient armies going to battle, two lovers kissing behind an Arabian sun.... anything! How do you think the Wachowski brothers done the Matrix? They had imagination already implanted in them from birth. They were Picassos and dreamers of their craft and it shows. You don't need drugs to access the visionary parts of your brain, it's already there. You do it every night when you sleep or when you get bored at work and your mind drifts. Imagine the feeling of illustrating something that only you can create; only your mind has the ability to depict, and not another single person on Earth can come up with the same look and feel you have when painting the brush of your imagination. Think about that. We all have fantasies...

yet these guys are expressing it to the WHOLE world.....millions of people sitting in dark theatres watching something, feeling the same things you're feeling, seeing the same day dreams you have when your mind wanders. That...is a gift. When you sit there with your best friends and your eyes witness the magic and blissful artistry of cinema's greatest feats it's a reward like no other. I'll give you an example that's choc block full of imagination-

The Lord of the Rings by Peter Jackson

No, not the digitally made immature pile of trash heaps called the Hobbit movies, those were a joke. Forget the Hobbit...whatever you saw in those movies forget it. They were dull, mindless, CGI half assed watered down garbage. THAT'S the truth about the Hobbit. But The Lord of the Rings...I'll tell you this much....what Peter Jackson brought to life from J.R Tolkein's mythology in the early 2000s was a feat no other Hollywood film maker could accomplish, Jackson pulled off the greatest fantasy epic and marinated it with a rich visual bliss that only a heavenly paradise could bring to your eyes.

The Lord of the Rings movies are in a league of their own and that's why the trilogy took home 17 fucking academy awards. Best picture, best director....you name it, Lord of the Rings got it.

Take a scene from the first movie where the fellowship, a hastily strewn together assortment of hobbits, a dwarf, an elf, two men and a wizard called Gandalf, are in the former Dwarf city of Moria which has been overrun by wild goblins. The fellowship are surrounded on all sides by these insidious creatures outfitted in body armour and armed with swords, and they're about to be killed when something even more demonic and terrifying hurls a loud scream in the distant emptiness of the underground darkness. The goblins lose their shit and run away because they know exactly what yelled in the deep. Gandalf knows, too, and lowers his head because the one thing he feared in these mines has come to greet them. Boromir, a foot soldier and prince, asks Gandalf very simply –

"What is this new devilry?"

Gandalf closes his eyes as the roaring continues while he answers very coldly –

"A Balrog...a demon of the ancient world"

The fellowship makes a dash for it to get out of Moria and escape the beast, but not before Gandalf is confronted by the Balrog. The demon spirit is a burning carcass of flame and fire, armed with a lava whip lash and horns as if the devil himself was as tall as a telegraph pole. The Balrog scene illustrates real imagination and visual excellence. I mean we're talking a masterpiece here, a trilogy that will last the ages. Not the kind of trilogy to go soft on epic hyperboles on screen, by the third movie audiences have already been drunk on watching battles from the previous two instalments...but in Return of the King....the whole scale increases. Want to know about epic battles? Let's talk about cavalry charges.

In Return of the King, the capital of Gondor, Minas Tirith is under siege by the forces of Mordor. The Orcs, trolls and Nazgul move in battle formation to attack the citadel. They have broken through the perimeter defences and are proceeding to rape the shit out of its defenders like any pillaging army should appropriately behave. Gandalf has assumed command of Minas Tirith and urges his knights to pull back; his commands are clear, fall back to the second level. And it's easy to see the concern in their faces as their survival is resting on a thread. Mordor's armies are huge, like a zombie apocalypse but well organized and properly trained. The concern riddles Gandalf; too, he knows they won't last the fight –

"Get the women and children out! Get them out. Retreat!"

The Orcs smell vulnerability in their enemy and like sharks encircling a bloody seal they go for the kill, hence the orders of the orc lieutenant in the battle –

"Move into the city. Kill all in your path"

They storm the city gates and flow through its streets and mazes like locusts, nothing can hold them back now. The human soldiers of Gondor fight like hell and high water; with every ounce of blood spilt they give not an inch. It's their final moments as their families await certain horror, and Gandalf makes it clear for each and every one of them

"Fight to the last man! Fight for your lives!"

If you were surrounded by an adversary bent on murdering you and everyone you loved would you pray in your hour of need? Gondor prayed....and got an answer...in the form of a really loud Viking horn. On the hills far away, towering over the fields of orcs and trolls, an army of Saxon-like warriors slowly converge atop of the plateau overlooking the city, their armour shiny in the early gaze of the rising sun, their spears long and protruding, among them a hobbit and a blonde hottie who tagged along as a lone female badass of Rohan. Turns out this blonde babe has an uncle who just so happens to be King of Rohan...King Theoden. Theoden inspects the shit storm before his eyes, gives a grunt like a pitbull and says in his head 'enough of this shit' before ordering his nephew Eyomer to take his company left and flank the enemy. He then tells his lieutenant Gamling to follow the Kings manner down the centre. And like any legendary badass who leads men into battle the king gives a rousing speech –

"Arise riders of Theoden, spears shall be shaken, swords shall be broken, shields shall be splintered! A sword day! A red day! And the sun rises!"

The orcs realize a bunch of gate crashers have turned up to the party and assemble their pikes in formation. Maybe they should have learned from Irish monks at Lindisfarme, don't fucking piss off the Vikings. The blonde shield maiden Eowyn whispers like a Valkyrie into the ear of her hobbit friend Merry

"Whatever happens stay with me, I'll look after you"

And the dude smiles, I know I'd smile too if I had a fearless norse woman guarding my 6 in battle. King Theoden swipes the front formation of spears with his sword, telling his men

'Ride! Ride now! Ride for ruin and the worlds' ending!"

The whole army roars 'DEATH' like a panzer division of car woofers and slowly trod the heels of their horses forward. The orcs unleash volleys of arrows to deter the charging horse legions, but to no avail...that's the moment the evil guys realize....they're fucked. The charging horse lords pick up speed, the symphony of violins rises, and what I'm documenting is perhaps the greatest cavalry charge in cinematic history. You wanna know about audience reactions in theatres? This one probably had the most lung raising, standing ovation reaction ever.

Imagine being a little kid in a movie theatre watching this unravel like I did in 2003....where everyone is so pumped that it becomes a stadium of boisterous elation. There's nothing that can compare with the epic scale of this...including that TV series with Jon Snow. Did you like Game of Thrones? Did you enjoy the horse charges and dragons with Khaleesi? Multiply Game of Thrones 200 times and you have the ride of the Rohirrim in Return of the King. And instead of cooling down, the battle increases the dosage when an army of tribal Arabs on giant elephants come to greet the Vikings. The rest I leave to your own imagination. OR you can watch it and get an over dose of visual mind blown pleasure from the greatest fantasy trilogy of all time.

Charge of the Rohirrim from Return of the King

On a serious note, the Lord of the Rings was also one of the few movies where eloquent and brilliant language is used, the type of language that Mark Twain or Abraham Lincoln would speak with. When I say eloquent language there's a particular scene in The Two Towers that really does breathe life into art. It's a father/ daughter scene between Elrond, high king of the elves of Rivendell and his elven princess daughter Arwen.

This scene I'm about to describe to you is necessary because it's emotionally haunting; it's a sombre reminder that our lives are short and we should spend every moment fulfilling it with the ones we love. If you have a girlfriend....love her dearly because this is a reflection of this lady's sorrow and loss. A bit milder than the epic horse charges I described but bear with me; this dialogue makes the trilogy have a lukewarm soft and ethereal touch. Lady Arwen is gazing her eyes through a curtain that breezes at night dreaming about Aragon, the man she is wildly in love with, when her father warns her of the impending doom –

"The ships are leaving for Valinor. Go now...before it is too late"

Arwen replies

"I have made my choice"

Elrond in a fatherly presence tells her very clearly

"He is not coming back. Why do you linger here when there is no hope?"

Arwen

"There is still hope"

He drops the news that would cut any daughter's tender heart right down the middle

"If Aragon survives this war you will still be parted. If Sauron is defeated and Aragon made king and all that you hope for comes true, you will still have to taste the bitterness of mortality. Whether by the sword or the slow decay of time Aragon will die. And there will be no comfort for you, no comfort to ease the pain of his passing. He will come to death, an image of the splendour of the kings of men in glory undimmed before the breaking of the world. But you my daughter...you will linger on in darkness and in doubt. As night falling winter that comes without a star. Here you will dwell bound to your grief under the fading trees. Until all the world has changed and the long years of your life are utterly spent."

The eyes of Arwen say it all; she weeps tears of sorrow on what will happen to her lovers' fate. Truly....this is one of the scenes as to why The Lord of the Rings is a masterpiece. Arwens fate makes any romance movie a sorry joke. For all the women out there heartbroken and torn from the loss of your companion, maybe you can relate to Arwens fate....

The Lord of the Rings or The Dark Knight, part of their crystalline beauty is that your eyes are trained on film. The image, the grain, the texture, the photo chemical artwork that has a dreamy feel, it's what celluloid delivers. If you like seeing the visually stunning then I have news for you....Hollywood has decided in the last few years that film and celluloid is no good. They've decided that celluloid hurts their wallets too much, because transporting film stocks to different cinemas charges them like wounded bulls. It's expensive to run and maintain film, not that it would take anything away from the greedy fuckers, but they're too money grubby to want to fork out for our pleasure. So what's a cheap substitute to them? Oh I dunno let me think....what cheap replacement can we use to simulate film but has a shitty quality and is cheap and affordable to move around the country? Oh I know....digital images!

As you already know, film is something that gives orgasmic fulfilment to the retina. So what's so different about digital? In as few words as possible....digital is a crystal clear perfect image. You might think that's awesome but let me explain.

A digital movie is so perfect that there is no depth perception between objects or figures. And depth perception is important because our eyes train to focus on it. Here's a little clue...when you put your finger in front of your eyes and you zoom in on your finger, everything around it becomes blurry. That's called depth perception. 'Films' have depth perception.

In 'digital' movies, there is no blurriness around the finger. It throws out gravity of the senses. So a painting on the wall behind the character in focus is just as illustrated, it's a one dimensional card board cut out. It's like watching TV in movies. It's flat and linear. Because when you watch a digital movie you're not watching tiny crystals contrasted together...you're watching 1s and 0s. You're watching numerals instead of captured images in a shutter process. I want you to read this and hear me out because I think it's important if we're ever going to have the magic of cinema again. It's not cinema if you're watching TV....you can do that at home. Digital is an image without substance, without charm, and I know because your imagination or your day dreams resemble the dreaminess of film. What do you want to watch; a dream brought to the big screen or a wild life documentary where every insect is carefully detailed?

So when discussing 'films' in the actual context of the word, yes...years ago Hollywood did have a nice contrast with its look and beauty behind them. So specifically speaking, what films had a mix of lurid dreaminess combined with good action, brilliant suspense and intrigue? Well to be honest, even most movies back then apart from the ones I mentioned were crap; there were cheesy comedies and stupid children's flicks. Movies are murals throughout the ages, they're not meant to be remembered for their immaturity or stupidity. Your art means the world, so treat it like the world. If there's one thing I can't stand it is light hearted bullshit. It doesn't matter if it's a stupid parody video on You Tube or a childish movie like Guardians of the Galaxy. If you're talented than God gave you that gift to put to good use so don't fuck it up and don't waste Gods' time with you. Despite the moronic comedy movies worth less than nothing, there is one particular director who has always been my favourite for his serious films. This guy doesn't mess around; he doesn't make shitty flicks about mundane and bland topics like your girlfriend's parents or the lives of your friends. So let me make myself abundantly clear...this one director makes classics because his films focus on quality and set pieces rather than characters and laughter. His films focus on history and historical stories, again another favourite forte of mine.

No it's not Steven Spielberg. It's not Quentin Tarantino. Not David Fincher and not Peter Jackson. Can you guess who it is, in my opinion the greatest Hollywood director of the last 4 decades? I'll give you a hint....he created one of the scariest looking creatures to be called Alien. Yeah you guessed it....roll the drums...the best director of Hollywood is Ridley Scott. It's widely shared by all pundits that Scott's Alien and Blade Runner are cult classics. I'll be honest I didn't like Thelma and Louise, or even Matchstick Men. Those movies were cheesy character comfort films. Ridley shines his brightest when he's dealing with history. As you'll discover later in this book, I too have a passion for history, the clash of swords and burning skies of smoke where the heat of battle burns over Stalingrad or Iwo Jima. Just as I explained how movies can portray your imagination on the big screen, history deals with a lot of that imagination as if you were there, sword in hand, blood soaked in the enemy's guts and hungry for more red. You were living that fight, tearing off that face, heaving forward in a cavalry charge with 10,000 horse archers under Genghis Khan.

The world is your oyster when you have a grand imagination and it's further made more enticing when you know your history. Ridley does just that, he's created some of the finest historical epics of the 21st century just with his imagination alone; movies like Kingdom of Heaven, Exodus Gods and Kings and Gladiator. You'll notice his movies are not too big on intimate character issues, which is what most American movies waste their time on. Because most Americans are sentimental and their movies reflect that (Ridley is British). Americans are too invested in meaningless horse shit like Modern Family where each character is a snowflake and everything is centred on their personality. Even though Modern Family is a TV series you get what I'm saying, when you look at US pop culture you see shows like Oprah, Ellen DeGeneres or Modern Family, things that are geared towards light hearted cottoned bud emotionality. Americans deal with things like sentimentality, empathy and character identities more than visual spectacles like Lord of the Rings or Gladiator. They think more about petty emotions than imagination. Even in their war movies like Hacksaw Ridge or We Were Soldiers, it's orientated around characters and what they're going through.

Whereas British directors like Ridley Scott have an eye for the imaginative rather than the emotional. Take a look at any one of Scott's films such as All the Money in the World, take a look at Prometheus or The Martian and you'll notice they don't warm with the characters but have huge set pieces instead that bring out the wonder rather than the chit chat. Europeans in general have a more imaginative outlook; including German director Wolfgang Peterson in his 2004 epic Troy, another visual ancient flick. The movie Troy is self explanatory, it's about the Trojan War between Mycenaean Greece and the Trojans. Wolfgang went little in the way of sentimentality, he didn't get lost in a web of intimate gossip on screen. Troy was straight to the point; Prince Paris is fucking the wife of the king of Sparta and took off with her in the night. Now the king of Sparta goes to his brother, Agamemnon, the supreme ruler of Greece, and stays their allegiance in partnership to invade the Trojans and bring that cheating bitch back for disciplining. Don't get me wrong, there were many characters in Troy coupled with brilliant performances by Brad Pitt and Eric Banner, but the characters were not lost in 'connecting to the audience'.

Troy was visually emotive rather than socially emotive. It's not common to see American Gladiator or American Troy but it's very common to see an American Legally Blonde or Meet the Fockers, because they want to feel with the characters. But you're missing the beauty of imagination. You're not meant to 'feel' a movie, you're meant to 'experience' a movie. They're windows into another world, not mirrors of your own life. I find Scott is one of the few directors with a fine taste for windows into other worlds. He's incredible with period historical pieces, the clothes, the sets, the weapons, the names, the locations; they're all beautiful in his movies, and to top it off, the look and grade of his films are second to none. When I speak of dreaminess, Ridley Scott illustrates a world that's straight out of the dream you've remembered since you were a child. Take the opening to Gladiator, a hand slides through a wheat field. The hallowing and mesmerizing chills of a latin voice accompanies the hand. The fingers trickle across the strands as children's laughter echoes in the background. The wheat scene sets up the world of Gladiator. If there's any movie intro that sticks in my mind...it's the opening from Gladiator, a portal into something ancient and mystifying.

By the end of the movie and a life of misery the sight of his wife and son under the plight of hazel skies, there they are, reunited in eternity. For those who have lost a loved one or a soul mate, if they were the only ones who gave you warmth and affection but they were taken too soon, just hear me out when I say the ending to Gladiator is probably the closest thing to meeting your beloved as one can depict on Earth. If you have seen the ending...or if you have yet to see it...it's a glimpse into the hereafter. And if its dreaminess and heavenly comfort makes you feel something deep down, remember why I prefer Ridley Scott over Spielberg or Tarantino because of endings like this one. Perhaps she is there waiting in those greyish fields where the wind cushions your faces and kisses the both of you the moment you meet again. The ending to Gladiator is something that truly touches your soul. The English director has an illustrious history of films meant for the ages, he hit the bull's eye with Rome, and he hit the bull's eye during another period in history much more recent. Another one of his works worth just as much love and integrity as Gladiator created a year later would, unintentionally, prophesize the future of urban combat in the Islamic world by American troops...Black Hawk Down. Not exactly sword and sandals, more like M16s, AK-47s and military helicopters which is where this film gets its name. Trust me reader...if you like combat classics you'll love this one.

Most war movies have a young man saying goodbye to his loved ones before being sent off to fight. In many war movies there are scenes of family time, where the main character probably makes love to his girl and leaves in the morning. Basically most war movies are sentimental piles of horse shit. Not Black Hawk Down. So if you're a lady and you love seeing a young handsome boy ride off into the sunset to fight for love and affection, think again, if Black Hawk Down was rated by feminists or liberals it would be 10/10 for violence, violence, violence and total violence....and I wouldn't have it any other way.

Black Hawk Down is the first 'true' war movie in the sense that its purpose is the pure carnage and murderous intensity of street combat. Although Saving Private Ryan did have the best depictions of combat and carnage, it was sprinkled throughout the movie. Whereas this modern war masterpiece is blood curdling from beginning to end. Black Hawk Down is based on real events set in war ravaged Somalia, circa 1993, where ruthless warlords are locked in a contested and bitter struggle with each other over territory. The most powerful of these warlords is Muhammad Farah Adid, who uses his power to seize international food shipments at the ports intended to be delivered to the starving Somali citizens. Instead of going to the people, he feeds his fighters, men of the Habir Gadr clan, who are based in the capital Mogadishu. When UN security troops are targeted and killed by Adid's militia the situation on the ground looks dire, so Washington dispatches its elite crack troops to hunt down Adid and put an end to the killing. The troops are part of Task Force Ranger, a joint operation of Delta force and the 75th Ranger regiment. In Black Hawk Down these men are portrayed by unknown actors who would later go on to play roles like Bane, Jamie Lannister and The Hulk. Leading a squad of Rangers is sergeant Eversman, played by the teen heartthrob Josh Hartnett, who has taken the duty to lead chalk 4 after his immediate superior, suffers a seizure.

Inside a canvas tent, Eversman, along with other team leaders are briefed on a possible op going down that evening. Major general William Garrison, played by Sam Shepard, informs the group that two top senior advisors of Aidid will be present inside the city. The two lieutenants will be headed to a meeting inside the Olympic

Hotel. There the Americans will conduct a lightning quick insertion by helicopters, snatch the senior figures, and in the confusion leave the city as fast as they came. Sounds simple. The mission launch codeword for the attack is Irene.

Hours later the task force is preparing their weapons and gear for the operation. Eversman briefs his squad about the approaching battle, with a rookie desk clerk tagging along with them, sergeant Grimes, played by Scotsman Ewan McGreggor who dulls an American accent as best he can. From a command and communications centre General Garrison monitors the city from satellite imagery above. He and a colonel keep their eyes on a white Mitsubishi patrolling the streets of the Bakara Market. The car is a Somali informant working for the Americans, and who knows where the meeting of senior aides will take place. At first he drives with trepidation as the market is infested with militia fighters drugged up on Kaht, a sedative that numbs its takers and prepares them for anything when going into battle. The car pulls up beside the Olympic Hotel and the Americans give the go ahead. The codeword for the mission is announced

"All units, Irene, I say again....Irene!"

You can probably check it out on You Tube somewhere, the Irene scene from Black Hawk Down which dispenses the tension leading up to one of the greatest battles in American history. The soldiers board their Black Hawks and Little Birds, lock and load and strap themselves in for one hell of a fight...cause they're entering the belly of the beast. Mogadishu was the most dangerous city in the world in the early 90s; it was a lawless town where only those with guns made the rules. Turns out the Somalis catch wind of the approaching American Black Hawks through a scout, and so the resident fighters of Mogadishu stock up on guns, ammo and RPGs. Imagine, for a second, a whole city where every person is armed with an AK-47 and hasn't had a feed in days. Picture how irritable for a fight they would be. That's where the Rangers are heading, they don't know it yet, but they're about to kick in the hornets' nest of some of the deadliest suicidal combat since the Pacific theatre of WW2.

There's a scene at night where the Rangers and a few Delta are trapped inside a building and are surrounded by thousands of die hard militiamen, there's no way they can fend them off just with M16s so they get assistance...from above. A couple of Little bird attack helicopters armed with chain guns hover above the battle. They radio Eversmenn down below and say they're unable to identify the bad guys due to too much activity in their night vision goggles. Eversmen says he'll dispatch a transmitter for them to locate and destroy the enemy. In an act of complete inconsideration for his own safety, the chalk 4 leader runs into the fray as his team members cover him from inside the building. He lobs the transmitter onto the roof of the adjacent structure and runs back to cover. The pilots are locked on.

Because October 3rd 1993 was no ordinary battle; soldiers were not going up against men in uniform who were well trained. They were going up against drug induced psychotics who were hungry, frustrated and bent on killing as many Americans as murderously possible. The movie opened just after 9/11 during a frenzy of American vengeance and would be planted in the minds of many young soldiers and Marines heading off to war. If you're sick and tired of all the flag waving conservative propaganda in movies but at the same time you're sick and tired of the emotional grieving liberal flicks when it comes to war...it seems every war movie is either conservative or liberal, well then Black Hawk Down is the movie for you that has none of those things. No pro American speeches, no clichés, no family time. It was shot in a smoky thick picture setting, so the graphics look grimy and dark. In my opinion, Black Hawk Down outshines Full Metal Jacket, Apocalypse Now and Saving Private Ryan. Witness probably the greatest modern warfare movie ever committed to screen that influenced video games like Call of Duty 4 and Battlefield 3.

The millennium era produced a slew of movies that encouraged masculinity and violence in its audience goers. That's what I love most about American youth culture of the time, teenagers and young people didn't have good role models, they had messed up role models including this next movie I'm going to tell you about.

Fight Club.

A movie this time made by David Fincher, where a young man named Tyler Durden starts up a street brawling club with his alter ego, and together they get their heads bashed in. Fight Club was the epitome of the late 90s; the dark sludgy graphics, the rejection of consumerism, the love of anger and violence. The movie begins with a flash forward, where both Tylers, played respectively by Edward Norton and Brad Pitt, are on a high rise floor with Norton strapped to a chair as Pitt places a gun in his mouth. The movies' storyline takes off with the real Tyler Durden, Eddy Norton, who is a bored office worker and is suffering from insomnia. Unable to sleep, unable to find any meaning in life, Tyler begins attending night time therapy sessions with cancer sufferers and Tuberculosis victims. It's at these sessions where he meets Marla Singer, played by the exquisite Helena Bonham Carter. Marla is a serial smoker and like Tyler, they're both posers pretending to have an illness when really they only attend these therapeutic communes to find some sort of semblance to their otherwise morbid lives. Tyler can't stand Marla, so during one meeting he pulls her up and says he's onto her, and if he has to he will expose her for her lie. Marla returns the favour by saying she'll expose him. Tyler now wakes up on passenger airflights to and fro across the country. A car crash investigator who inspects and records the effects of car accidents due to their faulty systems, during one of his mid air awakenings he runs into a stranger, played by Brad Pitt. The reflection of who he really dreams of becoming, the easy living, carefree soul who is cynical on everything about American life.

Since they're both the same person I'll refer to Norton as Tyler Durden and Brad Pitt as TD, since Brad's character doesn't have a name in the movie and using the same name would be confusing. Tyler comes home to his apartment only to find it has exploded with all his belongings and goods sent sailing into the night, thanks to a gas stove he left on. With nowhere to go and nowhere to bunk he calls up the stranger he met on the flight. After letting the phone ring out there is no answer. He leaves the phone booth when the phone rings back. He answers to find out its TD, the man he was looking for. They schedule to get together and grab a beer.

At a local venue the two men are drinking to their sorrows when Pitt's character laments on the negative and harmful effects of consumerism. How people spend their money on buying things they don't really need. And how it's a system to keep them enslaved and continue feeding into this machine. The two leave the bar when TD urges Tyler to ask him the question he's wanted to ask all night. After spurring him on, Tyler asks if he could stay at his place. TD agrees, only to ask him another favour. This time, he wants Tyler to punch him in the face as hard as he can. Tyler is shocked by the affront, and at first kindly refuses, but the other dude is adamant that he wants to get punched in the face. The two start fighting, in a friendly but grizzly manner, and so begins the origins of a Fight Club. Gradually as the two hammer into each other night after night they attract spectators. These middle aged men who watch them fight, themselves tired and spent from a life of corporate consumerism and raising families, join in.

For some Neanderthal knuckle head reason these people derive satisfaction out of getting their heads busted. They lament about the negative and harmful effects of consumerism but conveniently ignore the negative effects of getting bashed for no apparent reason other than to create an escape. It's just one big vicious cycle.

Eventually Tyler loses his office job, punching and sending himself through glass coffee tables in front of his boss. And eventually both Tyler and TD live in the same run down shack along with Marla. One of the testicular cancer sufferers, Bob, played by rock legend Meat Loaf, encounters Tyler on a sidewalk one night and tells him he's part of a secret club, he can't tell anyone it's real name because what's the first rule of Fight Club?

If you haven't seen it, it's definitely up there with the classics. One of the reasons I like Fight Club is because it's enriched with something you don't see in movies today...testosterone. Any movie that has badass characters is automatically cool in my books including this next one... The Matrix.

The Matrix revolutionized cinema just like sound movies when they became a thing, it changed the way people thought about the world they live in and how they interact with technology. What is the Matrix? It's a question that has been nagging inside the head of Thomas Anderson, better known as his cyber hacker alias Neo, and the main protagonist of the film. Neo, played by Keanu Reeves, lives in an apartment unit by himself and is searching for the answer to this question. One night when he is asleep beside his computer, dozing off, Neo realizes the screen goes black with the words appearing in green

'Wake up, Neo'

His eyes open and his looks at his computer, which now says

'The Matrix has you'

'Follow the white rabbit'

He tries shutting down the anomaly, when he reads

'Knock, knock'

Someone knocks on his door, astounded, he asks who it is when it turns out to be his friend Troy. He exchanges some sort of hacking disc with the dude who is outside with his friends. Suspicious, he asks Neo if he's ok since he looks a little whiter than usual. Neo asks him

"Have you ever had that feeling if you're awake or still dreaming?"

Troy tells Neo that he needs to unplug and invites him out to a dance club with his friends. He declines the offer at first, but when Troy's girlfriend turns he catches a tattoo of the white rabbit on her shoulder. That convinces him to go. In some Cyber Punk festival Neo rests beside a wall, alone in his own world as the music around him blares. That's when he's approached from behind by a woman. It turns out to be Trinity, 'the' Trinity who cracked the IRS D base, which was a long time ago in her words. She comes up to his ear and tells him the question he is searching for is out there, it will find him. The next morning he wakes up to discover he's fifteen minutes late for work and still in bed.

Back at his desk he sits when a Fed Ex courier delivers him a slip. He opens the packet to see a large brick phone fall into his palm and immediately rings. Neo answers. It's a cult-like figure in the hacker world – Morpheus. He tells Neo they're coming for him and he doesn't know what they're going to do.

"Whose coming for me?"

"Stand up and see for yourself. Do it slowly...the elevator"

Neo stands to see three men with black shades turn their heads in his direction. Morpheus guides Neo away from danger and out onto a window perch, saying he must climb a scaffold to get away. It becomes too dangerous and Neo turns back, taken into custody by the agents in dark shades. Inside a green tinted room he is questioned by the senior agent, Agent Smith, played by Hugo Weaving, the same guy who gave Arwen her life story, but in this movie talks a lot slower as if he was programmed. Smith tells Neo that he has been contacted by a highly dangerous individual named Morpheus

"Whatever you think of this man is irrelevant. He is considered by many agencies to be the most dangerous man alive"

Smith offers him an option, Neo assists them in their search for Morpheus and in return they will wipe his hacker slate clean. Neo instead gives him the finger

"Oh Mr. Anderson....you disappoint me"

"You can't scare me with this Gestapo crap. I want my phone call"

"Now Mr. Anderson what good is a phone call if you're unable to speak?"

He looks around at the other two agents standing on either side of him, when suddenly his lips are glued shut by some supernatural phenomena. With his mouth sealed skin they pin him on the table and Smith unveils an AI probing squid that crawls over his stomach and rivets itself inside his belly button. Excruciating in agony, Neo screams with a sealed mouth...that's when he wakes up in his bed from a bad dream. His mouth is still normal; his stomach is normal, the phone on the bench rings and he answers.

"Morpheus...what's going on...what's happening to me?"

Morpheus explains that he is the one, and that he has spent his entire life searching for Neo. He finally offers the question if he still wants to meet. Neo agrees and waits under a bridge that is trickling from heavy rainfall. A black car pulls up and Trinity opens the door urging him to get in. The car arrives at a large Victorian era apartment building with rain dripping down the architecture. Neo and the crew walk up a large flight of stairs. Trinity opens the door and he walks inside to meet Morpheus, outfitted in leather and round shades. The two sit down in leather chairs as Morpheus engrosses Neo in a conversation about human relativity and existence.

"I imagine, that right now, you're feeling a bit like Alice... tumbling down the rabbit hole?"

"You could say that"

"I can see it in your eyes. You have the look of a man who accepts what he sees because he is expecting to wake up. Ironically this is not far from the truth. Let me tell you why you're here...you're here because you know something. What you know you can't explain but you feel it, you've felt it your entire life, that there's something wrong with the world. You don't know what it is but it's there. Like a splinter in your mind driving you mad. It is this feeling that has brought you to me. Do you know what I'm talking about?"

"The Matrix?"

"Do you want to know what it is?"

Neo nods in confirmation

Morpheus explains that the Matrix is everywhere, even in that very room, Neo can see it when he turns on the television or when he looks out his window. It is the world that has been pulled over his eyes to blind him from the truth.

"What truth?"

"That you are a slave, Neo, like everyone else you were born into bondage, born into a prison that you cannot smell or taste or touch, a prison for your mind."

Morpheus leans forward with a pill in each hand; he offers Neo a choice between blue and red. Turns out that red pill were more appealing than the blue one. Neo is lead to a shanty back room and wired to a chair, the pill was a neural trace simulation that will access his location. As Neo looks to his right he sees the first anomaly in the Matrix, a mirror that's been warped. He touches the mirror and its mercury body slowly swallows his arm, then his body, then his face and travels down his throat. He wakes up in a tube, with plugs and ventricles anchored in his body. His head pipes up through a gooey surface where he removes a giant cord from his mouth. He has no hair, no muscles, and no memory. He looks out over the tub he is situated in to see thousands of equal-sized tubs that run up and down massive towers. Electric bolts sizzle up and down the city of human incubators. A nightmare like nothing before, he is freed and the ventricles rip out of his body, the shut opens and he swivels through a whirlpool of tunnels before falling into a gutter catch. A large clamp clutches his frizzled body and he is lifted into the heavens.

The next time he comes to life he is laid up in a bed. Morpheus takes Neo on a tour through his hover craft, the Nebuchadnezzar, where members of his crew work including Trinity, Cypher, Apoc, Switch, Dozer, Tank and Mouse. He finally alerts Neo to the question

"You wanted to know what the Matrix is?"

Neo is once again hooked up to a chair and told to relax.

A cable barb is inserted from behind his head and he screeches in agony before waking up in a dual reality, a completely blank space

"This is the construct"

Says Morpheus

"We can load anything from weapons to equipment, clothing, training simulations....anything we need"

Neo can't believe it

"Right now....we're in a computer program?"

"Is it really so hard to believe? The clothes on your body are different, the plugs in your head and arms are gone"

He sits down on a chair and the world changes

"Welcome to the desert...of the real. We have information in bits and pieces but we do know that at some point in the early 21st century all of man rejoiced, we marvelled at our magnificence as we gave birth to AI. Throughout human history we have relied on machines to do our work for us, fate it seems is not without a sense of irony. The human body produces more body heat than a 120 volt battery and 1500 BTUs, combined with a form of fusion, the machines found all the energy they would ever need. There were fields Neo, endless fields where Human Beings are no longer born... we are grown. For the longest time I wouldn't believe it, watch them liquefy the dead as they were fed intravenously into the living, and standing there watching the horrifying precision, I came to realize the obviousness of the truth. What is the Matrix? The Matrix is a computer generated dream world, built to keep us under control, in order to change a human being into this"

He holds up a battery

The young Neo refuses what he has heard, he awakes from the simulation and refuses to believe what they just packed his head with. Would you freak out if you just found out your entire existence was nothing but an artificial reality and that the entire Human race is enslaved? Neo can't take it, and he falls to the floor and vomits.

It was the sort of movie that had brilliant performances, on top of stellar action, shoot outs and sleek picture quality. Another brilliant performance by one of the actors was Hugo Weaving who played Agent Smith.

It's around this time that Neo, now fully integrated into the crew and mentally equipped with the last combat training, decides to go back into the Matrix and rescue Morpheus who has been taken captive by the agents. Trinity decides to go with him. They lock and load on weapons in the construct.

Smith is growing impatient with the interrogation as they're trying to crack into Morpheus' mind for the codes into the Zion main frame, the captain of the Nebuchadnezzar is handcuffed to a chair as Morpheus gives a lecture on the cancerous strain to the planet that is the human race. He tells him quite simply that we're a plague, a virus, and the machines are the cure. As he tries to break into his mind for the codes Morpheus is already on the edge.

That's when two leather boots calmly walk into the building with a black trench coat dragging behind them. The dude places his bags onto the metal detector rollers. The red line turns on. A security guard calmly confronts him and asks him to remove any metallic items he may be carrying like keys or loose change. The dude opens his jacket and reveals a whole arsenal of gats

"Holy shit!"

He karate chops him in the heart, pulls out two MP5s and starts blasting on either side of him, killing everyone in the way. Trinity walks in and blows the last sucker clean off da rectus scale with an Uzi. They grab their bags, drop their gats and pull out a new batch of shiny chrome burners as they make their entry into the building lobby. A whole crew of dudes in blue suits and M16s bear down on them, take up their positions and surround the two. Trinity and Neo look at each other, drop the case they was holding and duke it out with the tactical police. It's a slow motion montage of bullets and debris splashing into the camera. When they're done and the fighting is through, they jack the elevator system and make it to the top of the building.

Trin and Neo kick everybody's ass when suddenly the pilot transforms into an agent and walks onto the deck. Neo spins around with two .9s and begins blasting, missing every time. The agent pulls out his chrome and takes aim

Our boy dodges the bullets and leans back, but not before he gets clipped in the knee. The agent stands in the sun and cocks a gun when another burner is put to his head and Trinity is all like

"Dodge this"

Ka BANG

The agents still have Morpheus when a helicopter hovers beside their window. Smith for the first time is genuinely fearful as they stare down the spindle blade of a goddamn chain gun. It unleashes a zillion bullets a second and rips up the place, the floor sprouts up with funnels of water as the bullets ricochet and cut up the room into a fireball of confetti. Miraculously Morpheus is untouched; everything else is toast. The agents are cooked; Morpheus awakes from his slumber and makes a break for the helicopter. The rest is history. So the original Matrix film was like nothing else before or since.

2003 was an epic year as well. Other movies that came out dealt with modern atrocities like genocide. One in particular deals with the ongoing conflicts in Africa, where tribal societies are caught up in modern weapons and where differences end in slaughter. This movie documented the reality on the ground, an unapologetic and unflinching look at the horrors in Africa. That movie is

Tears of the Sun

Another classic war film up there with Black Hawk Down, Tears of the Sun was a about a squad of Navy SEALs who are deployed into Nigeria to evacuate French national Lena Kendrix, played by

Italian Goddess Monica Belluci who is working at a mission deep in the jungles. Lena is confronted by Lieutenant Waters, played by Bruce Willis, and told she must leave with his team. When Lena refuses and says she won't leave without her African patients then things become a problem. Waters promises her that he can evacuate all 60 refugees but first they must hike to the extraction zone to be picked up by helicopters and be choppered out.

When they get to the landing zone 'LT' takes doctor Kendrix but the SEALs refuse the refugees from getting on the birds. She realizes Waters tricked her into bringing her people only to show his true colours at the last second and snatch her in the confusion. In a fit of horror she is forced to leave her people she connected with, even though they may die at the hands of the rebels who have seized power in the country and are killing Christians everywhere. When they fly over the mission, Kendrix looks out to see the people left slaughtered and their bodies scattered across the camp in a sea of blood. The rebels reached the camp while they were hiking and murdered everyone in sight, the sick, the elderly, the young, the priests, no one was spared. Unable to manage the horror of what her eyes witness Lena cries hysterically as she knows the survivors they left behind are sure to die, with no help or aid from anyone, left to die at the hands of murderers. LT Waters will realize this fact, too, and in a brief moment of humanity, he rediscovers compassion and orders the helicopters to turn around to save the people they abandoned.

The helicopters return and take the vulnerable and the young, leaving the rest to journey with the SEALs to the next pick up site which is in neighbouring Cameroon. But hot on their tail are the rebels with every intention of killing them and the Americans. What follows is a movie that portrays the horrors of ethnic cleansing and tribal warfare, a movie that also showers America's military with the boldness and credit they deserve. And not one to go soft on action, Tears of the Sun distinguishes its moments of humanity and human tragedy with excellent battle scenes and explosive machine gun play.

I'm not talking about your average action movie; I'm talking about a film that puts you in the thick of jungle warfare. In case you want a glimpse of that kind of thing, watch the trailer for Tears of the Sun; a truly awesome trailer that mixes guns, emotions and humanity and what America's deadliest hunters go through to save lives

Tears if the Sun,

The movie was directed by Antoine Fuqua, in my opinion one of the best American film makers out there. Antoine has a track record of making excellent classics, and in 2001 he gave us perhaps the coolest bad cop movie ever made. If Grand Theft Auto was a movie and the main character was a rogue narcotics agent...the movie would be Training Day. Training Day with Denzel Washington and Ethan Hawke...let me tell you something, if you like street vets being more lucrative than the criminals they hunt; Training Day is that type of movie.

The opening begins with the sun rising into the morning sky, followed by one of the lead characters waking up in his bed. LAPD officer Jake Hoyt (played by Hawke) has a wife and a new baby girl, and today is his training day as a narc. The wife picks up the house phone only to hand the call over to Jake, it's the detective he'll be working with, narcotics detective Alonzo Harris (played by Denzel). The day will not be what Hoyt expects. His first encounter with Alonzo is at a coffee shop in downtown LA, the senior narc is clearly uninterested in getting to know his new rookie partner. Instead he stares into a newspaper, ignoring Hoyt's presence totally at the same table. When Hoyt annoys Alonzo he asks him –

'Tell me a story, Hoyt'

'You mean my story?"

"No not your story, 'a' story. Since you can't keep your mouth shut long enough for me to read my paper tell me a story'

'I don't think I know any stories'

'No? Ok, I'll tell you a story. This is a newspaper...its 90 % bullshit. But it's entertaining. That's why I read it because it entertains me. You won't let me read it. So you entertain me with your bullshit, go ahead'

after a long and tedious story about a DUI stop Alonzo is still unimpressed. However cool Jake might have been out on the streets as a valley patrol agent today will be a game changer for the rest of his life. The two leave the coffee shop as Alonzo strolls across a main road with no consideration for the cars coming at him. Jake follows the renegade detective to his Monte Carlo.

'Get in its unlocked'

'This car is not from the motor pool'

'No it's not, sexy though isn't it?'

He cocks a sleek looking silver 9 and Jake asks him

'So where's the office back at division?'

Alonzo turns and calmly replies

'You're in da office, baby'

Proceeded by one of the smoothest car scenes in cinema history. I don't want to spoil it, but let's just say the 1979 Monte Carlo scene from Training Day is one of the reasons Denzel was perfect for that role. The music, the hydraulics, the setting...just fucking badass. They don't make em like Training Day anymore. The rest of the movie is punctuated with twists, corrupt behaviour, shoot outs, gang intimidation, suave and just total badasstitude. Training Day is NOT a joke or a light hearted viewing; it's the type of shit that gets you accustomed to the mentality of American undercover in places of crime and betrayal. One scene that delves into that serious mentality is the following one

'What up dawg, you know where you're at fool?'

Alonzo comes face to face with a Cholo gangster as Hoyt and himself come to a party somewhere in south central. The two men walk up the stairs and they are looked and sneered at by a hood of Latinos blasting Cypress Hill. The Narc knocks on the door

'Hey I got some things for the family'

some dude opens the door and let's them in as they walk through the living room into the kitchen

'We rollin' in 2 minutes I'm just going to the head'

Alonzo walks into the bathroom

'Hey that's nice holmes, let me see it eh?'

'You got the CD player, the blenders mine. DREAMER! Get your ass in here'

Some latina hottie walks into the kitchen

'Make sure it's all there ey?'

'Next time learn to fucking count I was doing stuff, fucking puta'

A bald Mexican dude laughs with some other homie at the table. The man with the moustache throws a deck of cards at him

'Play it again'

'You play cards, cop?'

Hoyt is reluctant to get involved

'don't be rude Ese, we invite a guest and you standing up. Why don't you play one hand there you go'

Moreno slides him some cards

'What you guys playing?'

'We're playing a game, holmes, so why don't you tell me something? How long you been a pig?'

The two hoodsters break out in laughter

'I'm sorry I meant a police officer, how long you been a police officer that's what I meant'

'I've been a pig for 19 months?'

'Is that right?'

'That is right'

'And you like it or what?'

'Should have been a fireman, I need one more'

'What you got dawg?'

'3 of a kind, 3 Jacks'

Sniper explodes with joy

'BAHHHHH Booyah baby! Wo hoo! 2 pair!'

Smiley, the alpha of the 3 shuts him down

'The fuck are you doing sniper? Porke won'

'Smiley, I got 2 pair!'

'3 of a kind beats 2 pair you fucking dumb truck'

Sniper can't believe his eyes

'Serio?'

'Serio holmes. Ey you fucking stupid ese, why don't you take your medication or something?'

Dreamer, the chubby hot Latina babe walks back in with the money in her hand

'Is it there?'

'If you don't believe me you can count it for yourself'

Smiley plants the wad of cash in the middle of the table between the 4 men.

"Alonzo pulled off a miracle eh? Times are tight, he scraped up a lot of cash"

"Who'd he jack holmes?"

"I don't know"

Hoyt is reluctant to answer over a previous event in the movie

"He jacked Roger"

"You know what the money's for? Alonzo, he's a hot head. Some Russian starts talking shit Alonzo just snaps. Beat his ass to death. Well it turns out that Russian was a somebody. Now, Alonzo he into the Russians for a million.

They gave Alonzo till tonight to pay up with his name still on the list. Nobody thought he could get cash that big. Good thing he got his blood money because there's a crew on standby. If he don't turn up downtown with the cash and not a minute after, your Alonzo, he's a dead man"

I know you probably heard it all before, crooked cop this, crooked cop that, but in all honesty....no crooked cop has ever been portrayed the way Denzel Washington did with Training Day. The whole structure of the movie was brilliant. From the very first opening shot of the sun rising over LA to the closing frame, I can firmly attest that Training Day will not disappoint in the slightest.

Moving away from crime dramas, now let's talk about monsters. This type of monster I'm talking about was re envisioned from a cheesy toy figurine and turned into a realistic, cunning, amphibian hunter that was capable of bringing a whole city to its knees. The year 1998 produced one explosive movie which in my opinion was the coolest most action-packed monster movie ever committed to screen; 1998 Godzilla. The Godzilla that looked sleek. 1998 Godzilla was a blockbuster hit, becoming the 3rd most watched movie that year in cinemas worldwide. The creature was radically altered from the original Japanese design to suit the appearance of a fast moving, digitigrade bipedal reptile that was swift, cunning and agile on its feet. Instead of a slow moving, overweight Humphrey bear, why not create a creature with a physical design that amalgamates strength, speed and hostility? 1998 took Godzilla seriously; it rendered its image into a carnivorous, motivated animal that was lean and shaped like a weapon. To me that's what the Americans took seriously over a comical and PG Japanese invented manuscript, and that's why it's a better movie than the Japanese ones. 1998 was channelled for the heightened atmospheric pressure of audiences that wanted to see guns, explosions, fire balls, cities burning and man unleashing the devastation of his killing capabilities. It was true to an amphibious hunter that lurked in the depths of deep ocean vassals in search of a place to nest.

The way it turned its head, sniffed its food, sensed danger and evaded helicopter attack from the sky and machine gun fire on the streets made it believable. The CGI is some of the best ever put to film, and far more believable than most Godzilla movies. The creature in 1998 was on the run, outsmarting American personnel and creating decoys where it would emerge from the background to claw Apache gunships out of the air and annihilate their retreat with acts of cunning and clever pursuit. Right to the point where the last pilot in formation dispatched to hunt the creature is led to think he is safe after losing its trail when the animal hoists up from below and chomps the helicopter in one fell gulp that incinerates its metal carcass and sends the propeller flying into the camera.

That's the pinnacle of a good action thriller, when the POV is smothered in fire and flame. Unfortunately the 1998 Godzilla version received a lot of flak and venomous hate from critics and die hard Gojira fans who had wet dreams about the original shitty toy design. But what they don't understand is that Westerners, most notably American teens high on violent video games and war movies are not interested in some Japanese overweight, rubber dummy, tail dragging cane toad that shoots magical rings from its mouth and moves like a lethargic yak drunk on a shot of bourbon. That would not scare a modern army with F16s, javelin rockets, armoured tanks and automatic weapons, seeing a large Barney struggling with its body weight to stomp on their vehicles. It's just not realistic. It might pass off today where digital movies incorporate fake looking goblins from Hobbit movies and unbelievable dinosaurs, maybe today it would work because today movies pass for any rendered garbage horse shit and slap stick it as a movie. But in 1998 there were 3 huge block busters, Saving Private Ryan, Armageddon and Godzilla. The beauty about 1998 was that there were no cry baby millennials and social justice pussies pushing for less action, less masculinity, less explosions and less violence, so you could smother your movie with as much violence, masculinity and action back then because universal wimpery and feeling sorry didn't exist. In today's world you probs couldn't press a movie past post production without filling equality quotas or some shit.

This is why it was possible back then to show American soldiers storm Omaha beach the very way it happened on June 6, 1944, to vividly and expertly reveal the grotesque disfigurement of human limbs and entrails as it happened. It was possible to make a movie about global cataclysm and impending doom with a space crew plucked from the ranks of the underclass. And it was possible... to invent a creature that looked like a Xenemorph from Alien but with reptilian skin and demon eyes. Anything was possible because directors used their imagination and not their feelings. Think about all the best action flicks from Hollywood; they all emerge from the late 90s and early 2000s. If there's ever one thing that needs to come back it's that time period, and the movies show why.

CHAPTER 3

Music of The Millennium

Skipping forward to the dwindling years of the early 2000s we come to 2003, it was this year that there was a song so dark and edgy that it honoured meaning and talent with fortitude and harrowing grief. The song could bring you to life...it might call your name and save you from the dark if you can't wake up. It has been reduced to an internet meme to find humour, but there is nothing humorous or light hearted about such power and resolute talent in an emotionally depressive and saddening tune. Do not ever take this song lightly, never mock its art or brilliance...for it is truly a 21st century masterpiece in the leagues of those such as Beeth Hoven and Mozart before our time. And I'm not kidding; this song is a legendary artwork crafted from the human mind to bless our ears. See with your eyes and listen with your heart's content to one of the greatest testaments to misery, edginess and despair –

Bring me to life by Evanescence

No one believed a woman could properly front nu metal bands that were labelled with testosterone like Limp Bizkit or Slipknot, a girl singing and fronting a hardcore rock band? It seemed like a joke. Girls didn't listen to hard rock; teeny boppers were more interested in Britney Spears and Christina Aguilera. There wasn't a market for women in a genre that promoted misogyny, roughness and confrontation. That all changed with Amy Lee; a young woman hailing from Arkansas, Amy was a teenage Christian singer at youth festivals when she ran into another teenager by the name of Ben Moody. They had a passion for rock, and they wanted to utilize their urge to rock so the two young teens formed a band. Playing at small time concerts and gatherings they forged a small following. Amy didn't just want to be another band; she had Gothic tastes and incorporated them into the image and sound they made. She didn't want an ordinary name either...so Amy and Moody came up with something that was picturesque...Evanescence. The word evanescence itself means to vanish or to disappear, like a ghost or a spirit disappearing from your eyes. Pretty cool name if you ask me. Lee thought so, too, and called her crew this new dystopian name. But they still didn't play in the major leagues. During 99/2000 the biggest bands on the planet were Korn and the Bizkit. They raked in the money by the truck load from their album sales and concert revenue.

Nu Metal was the last big rock revolution; the late 60s had the Beatles, Rolling Stones and Led Zeppelin; the late 90s had Korn, Disturbed and Slipnot. The late 60s had LSD and free love; the late 90s had baggy clothes, short hair and backward fitted caps. By 2002 nu metal was becoming more female friendly. Women rockers were the new trend, paving the way for other ladies of the genre.

Take like Avril Lavigne; a chick that went worldwide. Avril had songs that got young girls off Britney. Because every chick knows –

"Sorry girl but you missed out, what tough luck that boys' mine now, we are more than just good friends, this is how the story ends. Too bad you couldn't see, see the man that boy could be, there is more than meets the eye, I see the soul that is inside"

Sk8er Boi was the biggest thing on MTV and Teen choice awards, teeny boppers turned into wallet chain, baggy denim loving bad girls. I guess we should thank Avril Lavigne for clearing a path to a new age of female wonder women. Sk8er Boi was a music video that touted a rebel bitch with an attitude and the idea caught on. Watching the young Canadian make waves throughout American entertainment as she hopped on the top of a car with a mic and smashed the windshield glass with a guitar as police helicopters loomed above. It was something cool, attitudy and rebellious. Having young skater dudes video tape your face as you wailed to some ex girlfriend about losing her lover. The early 2000s took girl power and smothered it with a layer of baggy clothes, sexy attitude and backward caps while a female wolf led the pack. Limp Bizkit with a girly touch. What a time to be young and free and girly.

By the success from the young Avril Lavign, there was now a market for female fronted rock bands. Record producers needed a front woman but with something different; a different sound, a different image. They searched all over America, looking for that special something. A band with a completely original name, a woman that could blast you out of your seat; not with anger or suicidal hate but with confidence and radiance; they found that woman. They discovered Amy Lee. They discovered Evanescence. The band started recording in the winter of 2002; cold time for cold music. They took their time, vicariously assembling the major singles with temperance, mastery and brilliance. Amy poured her heart and soul into the songs she felt dearest to, giving them her spirit. Is it possible that rock can have a soft touch? Can loud guitars actually go well with a piano? Here's a song where brilliance constitutes the efforts of a masterpiece. When we go to Heaven, you'll be transported by angels singing this work of Amy Lee to your ears

My Immortal

Watching Amy in black and white lying on a Volkswagon as the leaves breeze across her feet, with her hands on her face crying to the world in a mothers' voice

'All the sanity in me, this pain is just too real, there's just too much that time cannot erase...when you cry I'd wipe away all of your tears, when you scream I'd fight away all of your fears, and I held your hand through all of these years, but you still have....all of me. I've tried so hard to tell myself that you're gone, but even though you're still here, I've been alone all along'

Their debut album Fallen has sold 17 million albums to date, a tribute to some of greatest music of this world. They exploded onto the music scene with an edginess and angst that was reminiscent of those times, just like the movies were dark and gloomy, so was the album Fallen. Linkin Park sold 800,000 copies of Meteora in its opening week of 2003; Evanescence emerged onto the scene the same year and took the world by storm. We will probably never get Evanescence again. As we move further into the digital age music will become more synthesized and less and less organic and fluid. Guitars will die off, both acoustic and electric, to be replaced by auto tuned synchronizers that blend sounds and material. It's the way of the world, there will still be talent and genius but that age.... that time that I just spoke of....it was once in a life.

I can only hope that as we move into an age of cyber electronic media and new age relativism there is a new product that will resonate with brilliance. It's easy to think that in this day and age we are losing talent, losing brilliance and passion. Beeth Hoven probably thought the same thing when his music was top of the charts in the 16th century, watching all these amateur hacks take notes out of his book and pervert it with their lack of genius. But there's a reason we remember Beeth Hoven, there's a reason we remember Michael Angelo, Michael Jackson or Mozart, the truly gifted souls that were touched by God to produce feats as never before seen. I can only hope in my heart of hearts that the world doesn't just become laden with mediocre artists. That it doesn't weigh down on musical genius or the ability to create something with an edge and a touch of perfection. There has never been a man such as John Lennon who wrote songs for the Beatles, we haven't heard something in this life such as Stairway to Heaven by Robert Plant and Led Zeppelin, there will never be a masterpiece of cinema like The Lord of the Rings trilogy. Audiences will never know what it feels like to watch Neo rise out from a tub with tubes attached to his mouth and body and have machines keep unborn children capsulated in red incubators. Watching and hearing those things, in that time and place, in that exact moment, in a certain period of history, that's why they were feats that broke through barriers.

Even though we are absorbed on Facebook and weigh our minds down with the drudge and drivel of social media sometimes I keep optimistic. I reckon to think ourselves that we have these devices in our pocket, small touch screens that fit squarely in our palms and are built for our usage. What if we didn't get bogged down on what somebody wrote on a status, what if we stopped liking and sharing videos, what if ignored all that nonsense and eradicated the disease from our lives that is social media? Instead of letting our phones rule ourselves every second of the day, what if we switched the tables of destiny and we became the masters of touch screens and iPads?

What if we swiped our finger across the screen and our Lexus started up and drove itself to our location in the street? By using technology as a weapon, not as a social addiction, you can become a vigilante of the world.

Think of the Ubisoft game Watch Dogs as you play the shady delinquent character Aiden Pearce. He walks the streets of Chicago with a smart phone in his hand and a mask across his face. Wearing a baseball cap and a trench coat he's straight out of the Matrix, he's part of the 21st century concealing a touch phone where he can hack the codes to any digital and security device across the city net space. We have the ability to break the IMF World Bank with these things, instead people use them to check up on someone else's boring table food or rant time. Video games are like movies, sometimes they're boring and generic copy cats that follow the same tried and tested pattern like Call of Duty. But even Call of Duty had something original like the first Modern Warfare. Call of Duty

4 Modern Warfare is considered the best game in the series because its campaign was original. It took the global war on terror and added a spin of nuclear catastrophe to the storyline. It was well written, well designed, properly made and carefully carried out with missions combining awe, action, suspense and tragedy. Other video games that have the rare case of originality is the first Watch Dogs, Aiden Pearce was a marked man; he evaded criminals and cops and kept an undercover zeal about himself. Watch Dogs was original in that it took a modern phenomenon like touch screens and turned them in decoding devices that could break into any program in a large city be it CCTV cameras, other phones with people's data, the police and their information. It was genius.

Instead of Facebook, instead of Twitter or Instagram or Snapchat, all these things are garbage to the mind and a complete waste of time meant to fill the pockets of greedy CEOs who profit from people's addiction to their usury on the internet. If your kids got off the social media mind grab and used the brilliant technology we could revolutionize the world in ways people would only dream to be impossible or unimaginable. Get off your feed....download apps that harness the motor from your Jaguar to rev up and pick up a stranger who was just stabbed and needs to find a hospital. Find software that allows you to see a 3 dimensional image of your car when it ran a red light and change the font so you don't get fined. Be a genius with modern technology, not a slave addicted to social bullshit. Just as Werner Von Braun revolutionised rocket technology, Steve Jobs revolutionized virtual technology with his invention of the iPhone. But it became grounded down in socialite dredge like Facebook. I believe Steve's vision was for a world where people could interact with each other and with objects by harnessing their endless capabilities. That doesn't mean taking a selfie every 2 minutes, it doesn't mean acting like an insolent brat on a viral video, it means changing the lights at an intersection so you can drive across the road when the other cars come to a stop because your touch phone has that power to change societal boundaries.

But don't be like Watch Dogs 2, where a hipster in skinny jeans and snap back makes the rules, Watch Dogs 2 was garbage because of those reasons. Compared to the original, Aiden Pearce was far more badass and scary looking than any wimpy character from game 2. Looking at the front covers of both Watch Dogs you'll see the first one was far more badass in terms of attitude and weaponry. Can you imagine Pearce walking around with generation Y clothing and chinos? It would be an embarrassment, that's what those cunts done to the second instalment. They gave the character a nice guy hipster appearance and it ruined the mood of the whole hacker attitude setting. Fucking hipster pussies...

If you like Generation Millennial skinny jeans and snap backs then brace yourself for the following sentences you wimpy grommet. I'm taking us back to the early 2000s and what you're about to read and watch will blow your fucking mind baby so stay tuned to good old Trav Daddy. Reverse the clocks back to 2003 and the Iraq war began, George W. Bush was calling the shots and Avril Lavigne was tearing up stages. Culture was on fire. Just like this next band that became the definition of 'hardcore'.

Are you familiar with the band Godsmack? If not, then crawl under the blankets cause your nightmare is about to walk out from under your bed. Godsmack is the type of band that would put millennials in trauma induced comas for the rest of their lives. The Boston band has rock guitars deeper than a werewolves' voice box, a singer with more testosterone than any action hero and a presence more fierce than solar winds. Just imagine bikers in the bad lands of Arizona making music that would scare the most murderous creature into a fear of being raped, this dude makes Megatons voice seem like a Chihuahua.

You want some of that ruthless aggression filling your tofu eating stomach? Well heed my words and witness the theme song to Scorpion King Movie, pay respects to the Godsmacks –

'I stand alone'

When you're in a dark forest at midnight....just think of that song and you'll do fine.

Godsmack is so freaking hardcore they make hardcore itself seem soft. The band was forged in Boston, Massachusetts, a city already known for producing knuckle breaking badasses like Mark Whalberg. I don't know what it is about Boston but the city seems to produce a tough people. I can't imagine its people wearing skinny jeans and listening to soft ass shit. That's why Boston was perfect for creating a band like Godsmack. So when the Boston Marathon bombings happened its police and law officers shot up entire fucking city streets with the bad guys.

Godsmack is not actually a Nu Metal band despite being around at the genres peak. Smack is actually a pure heavy metal band, because there are no turn tables, rapping or down tuned guitars. The guitars are actually heavier and fiercer than those of Korn and most nu bands. Sully Erna doesn't scream into the microphone, there's no senseless cussing and loss of frustration like scream music. Godsmack was pure....PURE heavy metal. If you don't like Limp Bizkit, can't stand Korn, not interested in Slipknot or you don't like heavy music in general atleast give this a try and see how the Smack differs from most bands of the early 2000s. Either by music videos or Spotify, check these babies out and see why they put the Lords name in smack. Give these next two a listen and remember Boston strong –

A GOOD DAY TO DIE AND CRYIN' LIKE A BITCH

Music of all types and genres was sensational in the early 2000s, which included RnB, Pop, Hip Hop and club music. You walk into a club today you hear garbage. You try dancing on the floor and they play shitty music made by some incompetent hack. When was the last time the 2010s produced a good club song? You know, like really got you moving and made you feel like MJ on the stage? Think long and hard because if you cannot remember the last time you partied to a good song with vibe and feel then allow me to explain the disco section of this chapter. Are there still young men in music videos with fade haircuts, ear pierce diamonds and good clothes that glow in the camera? I know the 70s had the BGs, but what do we have today? Are we really Stayin Alive?

Because I got news for you, club music today sucks big time. All those idiot rappers with lyrics about how many cars they have, how many women they can pull, how expensive their latest jewellery is. Come on, you know as well as I do that such music is the equivalent of garbage. Like I said before the 2010s produced brilliance with touch screens and iPhones, those things are an act of genius. But perverted in the wrong way they become social addictions. Club music was genius but now it's been perverted into a stupid annoying trend that people don't even feel or vibe within their blood.

I'm not saying the 90s had the best club or rave music either, because there was a lot of crap back then too. There has always existed puny music, songs with no real talent or meaning or feel goods. The 2000s was my kind of era when it came to RnB and club. Despite the crappy songs that were produced there was also a trend of really cool music going around. One dude in particular became the hallmark of clubbing and mingling with pretty babes, this young man had everything; the looks, the skill, the talent and the voice. I can't say the same thing today because he's a fully grown man but as a youngster he had fire. His fire was ignited and he showed the world his dance moves and how agile he could gel.

Michael Jackson was good for the 80s, but glittering tuxedos and curly hair never went well in the early 21st century. This next dude was perfecto for the 21st century; he slowly emerged from a boy band and went solo. He dropped nice guy lackey personas for bad boy b boxing. Do you know what sleek means? I mean the guy was fresh as fine water and totally sleek in music videos, able to pull any girl at 23 and do it with ease. I'm jealous bro; this guy was cool back in his heyday. So let me share some notes from of my favourite beats from him and see if you agree about talent and cool kiddery –

'Don't be so quick to, walk away, dance with me; I want to rock your body to the break of day, come dance with me'

Everyone from home gurls and O dogs....rock your bodies and remember why the 21st century needs young JT back. Mr. Timberlake was the best RnB dancer of those years, making music that was jiggy and kick ass with a style that was cool, and a good role model for young men. He made music that was enjoyable, fun, entertaining and most of all...talented. That's something very rare you find these days. He made other great songs like 4 Minutes to save the world and Cry me a River. But in Rock your body he's got the haircut of a smooth talking, sleek dancing, prolific beat boxing grand master.

He was around at a time where both men and women were in tune with their instincts. Just like Nu Metal and pop punk were opening roads for young women so was dance music. This next babe I'm describing was a young honey that became the sexual Goddess of the 2000s, I mean sexual Goddess bar none. No woman in Heaven or Earth could touch this baby because if Venus came to visit mankind her name would be Christina Aguilera. Xtina made headlines and shocked critics and fans alike with her theme song that would define an entire culture, because Aguilera wasn't just sweet and lovable, she was Dirrty......

'Move, I'm overdue, gimme some room, I'm coming through'

Dirrty is a song your grandparents would have a fit over

In 2002 Christina was young, flirtatious, rowdy and her music showed it. Songs like Dirrty and Can't hold us Down became successful hits that empowered young girls to wear their cut jeans loud and proud. Her songs were voracious and her voice has one of the most resoundingly powerful cords known, up there with Amy from Evanescence and Adel years later. The all American sweetheart next door was now inserted into the minds of every young male. More so than Britney, Xtina was every teenage boy's fantasy. But apart from her there was one female group who were definitely in the minds of boys, a female group with attitude and girly badassery.

We're moving into the mid 2000s now but bear with this paragraph, the culture and mentality was still the same. A girl group injected with too much sexual oestrogen, ladies with asstitude. Yeah that's right....The Pussycat Dolls. These pussies were the hottest thing on the charts during the 2000s. And while there have always been girl groups like the Spice Girls and Destiny's Child, the Dolls were the first ones to be rebels with their paws.

I don't 'Hate this part' because 'When I grow up' I want to be unzipping 'Buttons'. The Dolls made proper music. The Dolls are the type of babes that would grab a man by the balls, pull him in close and say

'I want you'

know what kind of attitude I'm talking about? All their songs by got them being super rejecting of men or being super sexy. The Pussycat Dolls were proof American women are the baddest bitches on tha planet! When I'm looking for a girl, I want a babe that resembles the hotties in –

Don't Cha

I know the Americans are responsible for the majority of music and entertainment that was released back then, as they are today, so let's shift the equation to another Western country. Just like the Pussycat Dolls, this group of bad babes were in a style of their own. These British hunnies had a talent and singing voices that matched their heavenly name. I'm talking about Britain's finest....All Saints. All Saints had singles that put your head to rest when you were alone and in the dark. Their songs could ease your pain, cushion your festering heart and make you fall in love with each of these gorgeous angels. Truly....they were gorgeous and their music mirrored their effervescent bliss. You probably don't believe since words cannot explain...so see for yourself. Seriously, I'm dead serious....let this song bring lukewarm honey topped refreshment to your soul the way Aphrodite would when she blesses her lover with the gift of affection –

Pure Shores by All Saints

Its tranquil touch gives a slice of heaven where the waters are crystalline and joy is plentiful. All Saints were gifted, when they weren't singing melodies about swimming closer to you, they were making other songs about love and friendship. But just like the Pusycat Dolls, women in music bring the beauty and passion of their bodies into the picture; they know they have an angelic bliss and that can ensnare the lusting eyes of young men easily. Women have the ability to use their bodies as eye candy, as did this next young girl. One song made by a pop princess dominated the world; the sight of her celestial body was like a poisoned arrow that emancipated your heart. A video where she is taken from the ocean and plotted on a rocky ledge, if you see this young honey gifted with Arabic and Latino blood mixed with a great body and heavenly voice –

Wherever, Whenever by Shakira

Watching her immerses the viewer in another world far removed from the horrors and tragedies of this one. Shakira seems to be the only person inhabiting a far reaching planet where the sun illuminates the horizon in a thick haze of love and indulgence in whenever. It's actually ironic that she has Arabian and Latin blood, because those two people are actually related by blood. We'll get back to music in a moment, but first let me explain something...

The Arabs are a Semitic people like their Jewish cousins, there's a lot of hatred between the two, but the blood of Abraham flows through both of them which means their genetics are intertwined. The Arabs and Jews had fought against each other and bred with each other for thousands of years, even the Qur'an states that a

Jewish woman named Saffiyeh is a 'Mother of Believers'. I'm not stoking sentimentality here, I know you guys are at each other's throats and that Palestine belongs to the Aliens, but hear me out. The Arabs also have a third blood brother.

During the Islamic rule of Spain for 700 years in Al-Andulis, the Muslims mixed and bred with the local Hispania populace, the Spanish. By 1492 the Spanish Reconquista evicted the Muslims out of Spain, and the surviving Moors were forced to convert to Christianity. Basically all of southern Spain had Arab and Berber blood, do the math....1492 was the same year Columbus discovered the Americas. These Arabized Spaniards conquered civilizations such as the Aztecs, Maya and the Incas transferring the blood of the Arabs into the local Mezitos. Over the centuries these multi racial people came to be called Latinos. The next time your Latina girlfriend wants to kiss you, look closely into her eyes. Look at her olive skin, you're not just looking at an Aztec, you're seeing the bloodline of Arabic beauty. Look at Arabic pop stars like Nancy Ajram and Haifa Wehbe then look at Latina stars like T Lopez and Adriana Lima.

There's an eastern blood in all of them. Moving over to Hip Hop most people remember Slim Shady from the early 2000s, Slim dominated the world of rap back then. But there is another hip hop artist whose music was just as good, a rapper whose music was straight from the neighbourhoods of down trodden New York. I'm talking about my man Nas.

When history looks back at rappers they see figures like Tupac and Biggie Smalls, but Nas is perhaps a better lyricist than both those men. You've probably never heard of Nas because he wasn't martyred through death, but his legendary rhyming capabilities are second to none. Try songs like 'It ain't to tell' and 'I gave you power'....the latter being the main inspiration for Tupac's 'Me and my girlfriend. Try songs like 'Film' and 'War is necessary' which are true testaments of New York street crime. Nas is one of those rappers from the 90s who survived the violence and made it to today.

Lately he's faded into obscurity but it would be awesome to see him return to the mainstream hip hop world and obliterate these fake losers claiming to be rappers today. Imagine an MC with the flame and lyrical murder like Nas straight slaying modern garbage. That would be a sight to behold.

He also made songs for the kids....songs that showed they didn't have to be criminals but could rule the world....a song like 'I can'. I Can showed that getting ahead in life didn't mean blaming the rich or blaming someone better off than you. It showed that getting ahead in life came all down to your own belief in yourself, just like the chorus goes

'I know I can, be what I wanna be, if I work hard, I'll be where I wanna be'

Anyone who ever got ahead in life didn't do it by making a scapegoat, they done it by the words of that very chorus. So give it a watch and see for yourself one of Hip Hop's finest –

I Can by Nas

Now there is another rapper from New York who emerged early in the century whose music is some of the most cold blooded, murderous and unforgiving rhymes ever laid on a track. Whatever you're thinking double that in terms of horror. I know Hip Hop has lost its culture and that it's a far cry from what is used to be in the 90s, but this rapper has made songs that even put the savagery of Tupac or Biggie to shame. What I'm trying to say is that what I'm about to show you is not Hip Hop, it's an artwork that deals in nightmares and horror situations of the most deranged. Hip Hop stories have never been told in such a way like what I'm about to explain.

Immortal Technique

Technique and his music has nothing to do with money, fame or luxury....his songs are too complex for that shit and are about as compassionate as the serrated teeth of a hyena, songs which are endemically brutal in their delivery and nature. There is absolutely no political correctness or garbage music in his first two albums, Revolutionary Volume 1 and Revolutionary Volume 2. Think of songs that get you thinking, get your blood boiling or make you feel a sense of loss and horror, songs that really cut deep in your flesh. Please, whatever notions on Hip Hop and rap you have, whatever you think of men bragging about drive by shootings or having a thousand bitches, forget all that, just forget it, then I kindly ask you to patiently and carefully listen to this song-

Dance with the Devil by Immortal Technique

CHAPTER 4

A History of Warriors and Prophets

Today America is at war with itself, a new civil war is taking place. Today resides a social disease called liberalism; liberalism is an ideology wherein its adherents think its ok for men to cross dress in public and be proud about it. It's now a country where it worships cross dressing perverts and gender neutral depravity. The post modern media glorifies transvestite individuals, broken men who have lost touch with their own masculinity. These people should not to be praised on television networks for their false sense of bravery.

This level of depravity is destructive and I see that millennials my age support such moral apathy. Because the future belongs to the youth, when you have youth thinking depravity is something fantastic, when they idolize genuflecting to deviant sexual minorities in the mass media than the youth have already destroyed the future. This is important to read, this book is about a music and culture period but we'll have nothing if we continue walking down this mindless track. Western societies are morally deteriorating at an ever increasing rate and if it goes unchecked then start imagining a horror society that legalizes and condones paedophilia. Don't think this won't ever happen because it will. One acceptance of lifestyle will lead to another and soon we will lose all sense of our virtues and integrity. Paedophilia and pederasty will become every day norm and even idolized as a special bond like the days of classical Greece.

That's because past societies started out strong but deteriorated over the span of a few centuries into a bath of hedonism and apathy that went unchecked. In fact it happened as recently as the 1920s in Berlin. One of the reasons the Nazis came to power is because of the debauchery and collusion of the citizens of the German capital. Paedophilia was rampart, hedonism, lust, it was out of control. Hitler put a stop to the madness and found the source of the problem being the left wing communists who proposed that anything goes, they were destroyed, their books burned, their art desecrated and the city was born anew as a National Socialist capital with conservative and traditional values.

The Bible speaks of a time where depravity and vice were exalted by citizens in Sodom and Gomorrah. Weakness and decadence had completely saturated those cities according to legend, and whether you believe the myth is irrelevant, what matters is the moral of the story (mind the pun). God became so disenfranchised with his children in Sodom and Gomorrah that he asked Lot to find him 10 good men; just 10 moral men and he would spare their complete annihilation. The imagination of what was being permitted in those places boggles anyone's moral compass. When Lot couldn't even locate 10, God asked him to find one. When he failed to find one, God unleashed vengeance and decimated the cities' where immorality was practiced as sacred and upheld as holy. Immorality will always be judged, and for all the compassionate souls out there offended by judgement of the decadent, go put a bandaid on your feelings. Cause it isn't going to stop any time soon. The world is run, organised and maintained by the hard, not the weak.

In 800 BC, when the same thing that is happening now in the West was emerging in Greece, weakness was taking priority over strength and survival. Soon it corroded all their qualities and cities like Athens and Corinth became centre points for men marrying little boys. This insanity slowly worked its way into the Greek way of life and soon nearly every city state was proudly expressing its sinful collusion. But as with all Humans, there are the weak and then there are the hard. Concerning classical Greece when weakness seemed to be the trend of the day there was one state that refused to accept depravity and moral sickness. This city state is perhaps most well known around the world due to its enigma of a war structured society, the city of Sparta.

Unlike the Athenians who married pubescent male children and condemned women to a life of solitude inside their own houses, Sparta was regarded in fear by the rest of Greece. That's because they were the only ones who were actually normal. As moral relativism suffocated most Greek societies the Spartans realized people were losing their brains and their principles. Then one day a law maker called Lycurgus sometime in the 8th century BC changed the very foundation of Spartan society.

He decreed by law all male borns who were pure blooded citizens of Sparta were to undergo a fierce and rigorous combat program once they reached age 7 called the Agoge. The institution was built to mould young boys into hardened killers and wilderness survival experts in the case of invasion, famine or some other disaster that was left to the protectors of the state. But Agoge also served a different purpose; it taught males to refrain from passion, vice and sin, it taught them unity through pain, suffering, hard times and misery. That is the only time when men should be bonded, not through romance or lust but by brotherhood through struggle.

This brotherhood exists to this very day whenever our soldiers go into combat and survive by watching each others' backs. It's a brotherhood that cannot be explained by words. Yet the Spartans understood its importance and ingrained it into the minds of its citizens. Even the women were taught the importance of their husbands being fierce warriors and not weaklings who run off with little boys in the night to marry. The women of Sparta also had considerably more rights than other women of Greece. Spartan women were the only women who gave birth to men, as Queen Gorgo was famous for saying. Heck, while other Greek girls and ladies were banned from leaving their own premises, Spartan girls and boys were out in broad day light wrestling naked together. I fear America is heading down the same degenerate pit that existed in tales like Sodom and Gomorrah. Civilizations go through these cycles of birth which is where I come to my next point about a civilizations take over; the religion of Islam.

In in the 7th century Arabia was a lawless swath of empty desert where going to war was the only form of entertainment in the barren wasteland. But for the settlements like Medina and Mecca, people were in contact with trade routes from the Persian Gulf. The people there were not ruled by a law code, there was no regulation of sexual activity or public behaviour at lewd parties where alcohol was ever present and in abundance. The Arabs were heavy drinkers, fornicators, perverted hedonists and pagans who believed in 360 Gods. Men would marry little girls, fornicate with already married women and pederasty was common which in turn allowed Arabia to degenerate into a twisted form of degeneracy. It wasn't until a goat herder named Muhammad woke up to the surroundings of his people and how they had lost their way did they change. After believing what he witnessed as visions from God Muhammad set out on a mission to change the very world he was born into. I know it's hard to believe that the Arabs would drown themselves in liquor and fornicate with each other since none of that behaviour is present today in the Islamic world, because that's precisely what Islam was built to stop. Islam is actually a defence mechanism against debauchery, Muhammad made it that way to revolutionise the very moral regards of his time. He did the Arabs a favour by outlawing alcohol, adultery and even lending money on interest, since many Arabs were under the finger of rich Jewish interest brokers. Muhammad was perhaps the first person in history to turn hedonism and apathy around into a religion of strict moral guidelines.

People today call Islam a religion of violence, a religion of hate, they call Muhammad a war monger and a war lord who subjugated other tribes and slaughtered their entire adult male population. Truth be told....those things did happen, people were killed, heads were ripped the fuck off and whole villages were reduced to a pile of bodies, what's the problem? You offended cause the Muslims started out with behaviours that you find repulsive? It's not their problem, it's your problem you have too much empathy. Christianity preaches about peace and love but Islam was never born into a world of peace and love. The 7th century was one of the cruellest and most animalistic time periods during the dark ages, after the fall of the Western Roman Empire mainland Europe disintegrated into anarchy and superstition. There were burnings, witch hunts, civil wars, threats of invasion and plague and that's just in Europe. I haven't even started talking about the Middle East....let alone Arabia itself. In the Levant region, places like Turkey, Syria and northern Iraq, the empires of Sassanid Persia and the Byzantines were battling each other in a series of never ending wars that severely weakened and degraded both kingdoms. I suppose their people were intoxicated on drugs and heavy consumption of alcohol, too. The whole world was lost, from Europe to the Middle East; everything was corroding away.

Confided to the middle of all of this was a barren and dry peninsula connected to both the Middle East and Africa. The peninsula was inhabited by a rough and uncouth people with a gritty and guttural language called Arabic. The people of Arabia, the Arabs, had spent centuries steeped in blood feuds and tribal vendettas. By the time of Muhammad, the Arabs were already too far gone. Fathers would bury their new born daughters at birth, ashamed that a female in the family would bring misfortune. Differences would be settled bloodily, no matter how small or insignificant. Muhammad told his vulgar people to wage war for the cause of God, because during his time the Arabs would fight over something as inconsequential as a goat. No I'm serious, there was once a war called the Basus war where two rival tribes tore each other to pieces for 40 years over the theft of a camel. Real wars lasted anywhere between 120 to 200 years, longer than any European conflict and over reasons far more mindless. That's how ridiculously bloodthirsty these people were. They would fight over anything –

'You stole my wife? I go to war with your whole tribe, bring all your boys and all their cousins Habibi, we dukin it out on the sands of Madina'

Or

'Yo, you disrespected my deen by looking at me wrong, now I gotta cut your fucking head off and plant it on my dresser as a trophy, you alright with that?'

Somebody had to straighten these rough and rowdy savages out. The task would be given to one man. He was from the tribe of the Quraysh, this Sheppard moved herds of goats until about age 25 when he met a wealthy Meccan woman called Khadija. Khadija belonged to a family of nobility and her high social status was in deep contrast to Muhammad's lowly class. Which is probably why she loved him, records of the Qur'an and Hadeeth indicate the young Muhammad as very handsome. It was during this time, during his marriage to the wealthy Khadija when Muhammad became dissociated with the world around him. His wife was a rich woman and he had splendour but wealth and luxury didn't mean anything. He left all those things, put them away, and did some soul searching....retreating to the mountains and hiding out in a cave. Something sent him mad. He must have gone mad, or the times were making him go insane. He became disenfranchised with the social setting and the norms of the day. Basically....he searched deep into his soul to find what was wrong with Arabia. He became an introspective philosopher. Asking questions like –

'O Lord, most gracious, most merciful, what is wrong with my people?'

Like I discussed earlier, the 7th century Arabs were not exactly the nicest people. They weren't the most happy or content either. They were living in Hell. Hell not just because of the weather or the desert heat, hell as in they were drowning in sins and immorality like Sodom and Gomorrah. The Qur'an calls this time the Jahilliya;

the age of ignorance, Islamic terrorists today are always winging how the rest of the world lives in ignorance and we need the true God but truly....before Muhammad there was a real age of ignorance prevailing in his homeland. Paedophilia and child marriage was everywhere; getting drunk on a hundred bottles of Chivas Regal was trendy in a single night. Snorting the most powerful heroin was considered cool, killing your neighbour for past wrongs was justified and don't even forget about blood feuds lasting longer than most countries' existence. These people had one foot in the grave. It was a nightmare if you lived in those times and took a step back to see the big picture. Not one tribe, not 10 tribes, not a hundred tribes, everywhere from the Persian Gulf to the red sea. It's scary when you think about it. Well one man did think about it. Muhammad said to himself in that cold cave next to the fire –

'Look man, this has to stop. We're living in a prison built by the devil. He's made us slaves to our passions; we're shackled and chained all over. God has made me aware of this. I swear by God I will stop this immoral insanity'

Muhammad was living in Sodom and Gomorrah, his mid life crisis made him rethink everything including reality. Basically he was Neo in the Matrix, what he knew he couldn't explain, but it stuck with him like a splinter in the back of his mind. Those nights he spent in the cave asking questions, they were like the red pill scene between Neo and Morpheus, except it was with the arch angel Jibriel explaining to him about the world around him. I don't know if Jibriel appeared with black leather and shades but I do know Muhammad discovered something that night.

'I imagine you're feeling a bit like Moses....tumbling down the rabbit hole?'

'You could say that'

'I can see it in your eyes'

'The Arab people produce more warriors than all of Sassanid Persia and the total might of Byzantine Rome, but combined with a form of sickness, the Devil had found all the minions he would ever need. There are villages, Muhammad, endless villages where your people are no longer decent....they have become animals. For the longest time I wouldn't believe it, then I saw the horror with my own eyes, watch Shaytan corrupt their souls intravenously sucking the fruitful blood from their hearts. And standing there watching the horrifying precision, I came to realize the obviousness of the truth. What's wrong with the Arabs? Arabia is a depraved nightmare, carved out of the sword in order to change one of your people into this'

Jibriel holds up a leech sucking from his soul

'No....I don't believe it'

'I didn't say it would be easy Muhammad, only the truth'

'STOP! YALLA let me out....I want OUT!'

Muhammad ran home after spewing up from so much information overload, the dude was so scared and shocked he demanded Khadija cover his whole body in blankets. Seriously, it's in the book. He was crying telling her demons were in his head. Khadija slapped him across the face and said

'Be a man and get a grip of the situation. You've seen visions that makes you a prophet Habibi'

Don't ever think men don't need their women

This isn't a one off thing, throughout our history we've had people who questioned the norms of their day and were petrified in their awakening. Henry Ward Beecher forwarded the notion that slavery was immoral and wrong at a time when the American slave trade dominated the world. The ancient Greek philosopher Heraclitus was born into a wealthy family but renounced his fortune and retreated into the mountains. He became dissatisfied with the world around him. Moses was a privileged Egyptian prince until he woke up to the horrors of the Hebrew slaves only to find out he was a Hebrew himself. I'm going to talk about our horrors of the modern day later on, horrors you wouldn't even imagine. It's coming so expect a wake up chapter.

The prophet began his mission to cleanse his homeland of intolerance and immorality by being a street preacher somewhere in down town Mecca. He brought knowledge to the rich and the poor... to the sheikhs and the unemployed. The guy couldn't read or write, the pre Islamic Arabs spread their knowledge through oral story telling. But Muhammad knew his message would last down the ages so he hired an esteemed local scribe called Zayd Bin Haritha. Zayd could read and write and with bits of bone and rock dipped in blood he wrote down what this new preacher dictated with words, after gathering 100 people to his covenant the prophet began calling out the Meccan tribe for what they were...drunks, fornicators, child murderers and idol worshippers.

The Meccani Quraysh picked up and chased Muhammad out of their city. He fled north to another oasis town called Medina, which was at the time named Yathrib. Yathrib was a Jewish town, and it was the Jews that the Muslims directed a lot of their hatred towards, even today. Why you may ask? Why are Muslims so anti Semitic? Well maybe you should ask it a different way. Why were Jews dominating all the banking corporations and television jobs back then? You know, miss world Arabia had to answer to some sleazy Yahudi smoking a cigar behind the curtains. I don't hate Jews; I think they're a resilient warrior people related to the Arabs with their own tribal society like David and his clans. I'm just saying Muhammad saw their economic dominance and put an end to that shit, they didn't belong in his homeland. But before he could do that Muhammad had a bit of touring. Like any emerging rock star, he had to sign autographs and sign swords with an ink feather. At least that's what he thought. He was going to a small town behind the mountains called Ta'if. The prophet believed if he could convince people to follow his way of life then he could lead them away from their sins. You must remember the Arabs were consumed in superstition, ritual infant burial, tribal wars, adultery, gambling and drinking. He needed to cleanse these things because they were cursing his people. Today those behaviours are called Har'am.

Muhammad began telling the natives of Ta'if

"Yo man, it's not right to bury your daughters after they were just born. She's a human being too'

Or

'I heard you guys kicked that other tribes ass. That's cool, but so is this, you gots to give up your beef. You feeling me, we all is brothers'

The people of Ta'if eventually got annoyed with his constant moral relativism and so they stoned Muhammad and his adopted son Zayd Bin Haritha (the dude that wrote down his lines) the citizens of Ta'if picked up rocks at their feet and stoned the two men out of the city. Muhammad's stoning was so extensive that he nearly broke his leg; both men were covered in towels of blood. With nowhere to go and nowhere to find shelter they came to an orchard where a young Christian man named Abbas took them in under his wing. Abbas took Muhammad into his hut and dressed his wounds. He felt sorry for this man; all he was trying to do was save Arabia from a cultural phenomenon at the collapse of every civilization.

A lot of westerners don't like Islam's Muhammad; they see him as the centrepiece for all the terrorism in the world. If Muhammad was alive he probably wouldn't care about infidels or cleansing non belief because his people have been freed. Yes you read it correctly, they're free; Arabia, UAE, Qatar and Kuwait are rich beyond imagination due to some black stuff underneath their sands this whole time, Islam is a global religion and Haifa Wehbe is a smoking hot Goddess in Breathing you In. What more you want? Saudi sheiks are trotting around the globe in billion dollar yachts with hotties like Haifa and your mom, the Arabs rule! Viva La Habibi! But enough of the modern paradise we call home...back to the 7th century where there were no computers or luxury cruisers. The 21st century is a light years apart from the dark ages. Doesn't matter if it's the Lombards conquering the Franks or the Meccans fighting the Banu Qaurziyah, back then it was cut throat and you didn't have time to bleed. The prophet recovered after a brawl in Ta'if and made his way to Medina where he formed a small army and kicked out its Jewish inhabitants, mainly because the rental properties were too high and interest was a killer. After a string of successes he took over Medina and with an army of some thousands he marched back towards Mecca, his original home town, to teach them idol worshipping bastards a painful lesson in respect. He conquered Mecca soon after. So it's true, Muhammad was a war lord, many will disagree and try to downplay his role or say the enemy started it first. But the fact of the matter is all Arabs were savage, no one was holier than the next. The Muslims were no more bloodthirsty than Banu Nadir, or the Quraysh, they were all equally cruel and vengeful with each its own share of fierce warriors. The prophet had deep respect for fierce warriors; he encountered one of the fiercest to serve in his ranks, a man who actually started out as his enemy. During the battle of Uhud Muhammad and his army was defeated. The rival strategist was a sole warrior called Khalid....offcourse I speak of the legendary Khalid Bin Walid.

When people think of great Muslim warriors they think of Saluhuddin or Timur, but there's only one Sword of God. Listen to what I'm about to tell you. Khalid Bin Walid was born to a warrior family of high nobility; his father was a dual wielding blade-master and taught his sons the sacred arts of warfare. His brother was a well renowned horse rider; and Khalid became the God emperor of desert combat. He is regarded as the only commander in history to never lose a single battle, and he fought 200 of them in his lifetime. Remember the name....Khalid Bin Walid. But as badass and as dead killer as he was, this man thought about his actions that day at Uhud, he won the battle but there was something more to it. Our boy Khalid did some soul searching himself, he was a great leader but his people were suffering and nothing changed, along came a missionary on a quest to change the ways of the Arab. So what does he do? Does he keep fighting this preacher or does he join him on his prophetic mission to ail the withering conscience of the Ummah? Khalid had a big decision to make. He came to the prophet some time later and asked for his forgiveness, the lion of Uhud still knew how to be humble. The prophet rebuked him and said

'You have nothing to be sorry for Khalid, we are all brothers and I hope you embrace me as one'

Khalid embraced the prophet Muhammad and together they would never have a rift ever again. Turns out Khalid Bin Walid, 'the sword of God' as he was called, led the Caliphates' armies for years to come. He won Walaja, Ullais, Yarmouk, Muzzayah, Jerusalem and spilt so much blood that the rivers ran red from his victories. No kidding, the story of Ullais goes that before the battle Khalid made a pact with God. If Allah granted him victory over the Persians he would make the rivers flow with their blood for as long as the current could hold. Turns out not only did he win but he also captured in excess of 70,000 prisoners of war. The general had every one of their heads cut off and their bodies dumped into the rivers to fulfil his duty with God. Say what you want about Muslims but give them credit where it's due...they are loyal to their words between them and God. Before each and every battle this dude was so badass he would walk out in front of the army and beg a lone warrior amongst the enemy to come fight him. Every time they stepped to him he killed them and collected their head. He held it up to the enemy and said

'This is what will happen to you if you don't submit to God!'

Khalid Bin Walid should go down in history as one of the greatest undefeated champions at AFC...Arab Fighting Champion. Instead, your average school class in the west has no idea about the guy. The Western education system is messed up. We could be learning about undefeated commanders like Walid or Subutai. People are more interested in Facebook and snapchats but I say fuck that, I wanna read up on real history like Hannibal's war over Rome during Lake Tresimene or Eric Von Manstein's defence of Kharkov, that's real history. Sorry honey but your selfie smile won't be immortalized 2,000 years from now, only the names of the greats are remembered. At the time of Prophet Muhammad's death, Arabia was for the first time in its history unified into a single nation. A single people, a single brotherhood, the tribal infighting was turned into a confederacy of tribal super powers. Like taking 10 different ant colonies at war and making them come together, the conditions were right to conquer other people. The next successor to lead the Muslims, called a Caliph, was Abu Bakr, the father-in-law of Muhammad. After brief civil wars where some of the Arabs attempted to abandon Islam, called the Rida wars, Abu Bakr forced them back into circulation and launched Operations Marty's Blood. The newly formed Rashuydin armies had the latest Tiger cavalry units, archer battalions and battle carrier fleets in the Gulf. By the end of the spring their Blitzkrieg tactics against the Persians had led to the subsequent capture of more than 100 cities, 340 villages, 8 garrisons and the annihilation of 12 moats and fortresses. The Islamic conquests of the 7th century remain one of fastest expansions in Human history.

In under a hundred years the Ummayad Muslims reached northern India and were marching into China while at the same time coming up through Spain and Hispania to the west. The earlier Rashuydeens smashed the Byzantines, destroyed the Sassanids at Al Qadissiya and Ullais thanks to leaders like Khaled and Umar. Arab warriors wielded the blade and fought with a tenacity not seen until the Mongol hordes. The religion gets a bad rep today, and I can understand why. They don't conform to the 21st century and have honour killings. I don't think any of that was intentional, remember Muhammad was trying to save them, not enslave them again. He didn't want women in burqas but he didn't want them being crack addicts either. People see Muslim women as oppressed and constricted, but at Islam's core is the heart of a lion....an Arabs heart.

I know you don't see it. You think of them as modern savages who live in squaller and rape underage children but I see a deeper side....a hidden beauty. Do you want to know what I'm talking about? I'll be very frank with you. Khalid Bin Walid, Ziad Ban Haritha, Umar al Khattib, these people was lions and you can see it in the pronunciation of their names if you use enough flem in your throat. Yes they were ignorant and primitive, but at a time such as the Dark Ages and in a desert like theirs, with the monstrosity of their social conditions, they were bound to fucking ignite. Operation Martyr's Blood went into full effect, and it wasn't just made up of men either, it had Arabian Shaheeda slayers too. Imagine if the Sword of God had a female version. Like warrior princess times a trillion. Do you think there was such a woman? Well....allow me to introduce you to the legendary huntress

Khawlah Bint Al'Azwar

The veiled, triple incisor carrying, merciless eyed Arabian woman born to kill pussies like you. This bitch was bad news, think wonder woman with a death wish. During the Rashudeen conquests where they were taking out every object from the Negev to Persopolis, our fine warrior leader Khalid had a bit of a problem. It was a mathematical problem he couldn't quite figure out. How do we defeat the Persians and the Romans while my army is sore, tired, bruised, hungry and exhausted from so much ass kicking? Well he went to the canvas board in the tent and carried out some equations.

'If I can flank Yazdegerd and his men on their southern front that opens a gap for my cavalry to come in from the east, but that still doesn't show an opportunity how to defeat their immortal battalions, damn it. I wish I had someone who could swing the lash of one sword and break their entire division.'

Khalid retreated outside of the tent and washed his hands when he looked up to see a lone warrior with fragrant hair beating up 3 men with steel chairs. The commentator to the match was J.R from WWE

'Bah God king, she's killing them! Look at her move those fists! She's parted the red sea with their blood, my almighty! Heaven save us'

'Oh no don't do it, don't do it, think of your family. Think of your friends. BAW GAWD SHE BROKE HIM IN HALF!'

For further details on this deadly match between Kawlah and the boys go to any Jim Ross commentary on the internet lol

Even though she was covered in blood she was still more beautiful than a thousand newly wedded virgins under an oasis palm grove. She had the type of radiance a man wants in a companion; confidence, courage, modesty and determination. Not the ordinary diva and not your average throat cutter. She had a streak of vengeance not to be messed with, but she had a heart to be upheld and valued with true men's loyalty. Whenever this Arabian warrior queen walked onto the battlefield she didn't do it screaming how tough she was or how fierce her ability was known for. Wanna know how she did it? Azwar had pink lavish handles on her blades and fluffy white fur on her legs and arms. As enemy warriors got pumped up with adrenaline, she would strut out to the front and kindly blow them all a kiss. Then it was game time.

However if you committed an act of great wrong doing that all changed. During the battle of Sanita al'Uqab her brother Deraar, another fierce killing machine, was taken hostage by the enemy Greek soldiers. Khalid and his elite Shuhaaha guard went in to save him but their efforts were futile. The enemy ranks were too numerous in number. Just as Deraar was taken to be beheaded over a tree stump, Kawlah realized her sibling was injured and missing in battle. Instead of weeping and begging the others to do the fighting, like a lioness she got on a horse, ripped out the longest lancer in the caliphate and proceeded to go on a blood induced rampage with the havoc and destruction of a whirlwind sent by Jupiter's red spot. The end result? An entire battalion of Byzantine soldiers laid dead and wasted, clasping for their guts between their finger tips and begging for mummy like that kid on the beach in Saving Private Ryan. This was Saving Brother Deraar....and just as bloody as Omaha beach. She recovered her long lost sibling and brought him back to safe ground. Not long after she was captured herself in battle and brought to some douche bag snorting cocaine in a big tent. This loser, who was named by Islamic accounts as Scum Cutty, was feeling fat and wasted from the drug intake and wanted more flare in his meaningless Soprano life. So what does he do? Khawlah was sitting in the corner like a modest woman thinking about how badass Walid was with his conquests when this dude spoke to her. Cutty told our home gurl –

'Hey, hmmmm, arrggh, mmmmmmm, I want you to urrggg damn that coke was thick'

'You want me to what?'

'I want you to uhh, smmmm, hmmmmgrrh, strip'

'What?'

'I want you to strip 4 me, do a little dance, be a good little belly princess for daddy'

'I don't dance for sleaze balls'

'Tell me sumfin I don't know baby'

Our warrior honey got agitated with this lump of shit

'Look motherfucker you got about 3 seconds before I take off these panties and turn them into razor rags with poison'

'Please, I'm waiting'

'That's it I'm out'

She got up and walked out the door. But the obnoxious toad ran after her and dragged her by the hair back into the tent. Being the take-no-shit from anyone kinda person she was, Khawlah twisted around and bent his elbow up then head-butted the dude back to Jerusalem. Then she left the camp while it burned down behind her like the Modern Warfare 2 cover.

The Arab Muslims of the 7th century were raised in the blistering heat and sun, made to labour their livelihood through struggle and hardship. That harshness birthed a people who were some of the fiercest and most rigid this world has ever seen. In a desert like Arabia with no abundance in luxury or wealth, weighed down by social immorality and plagued with constant warfare, in a time period where every culture was losing its way, the Arabs had the raw end of the stick. One man picked them out of the grave, surrounded by loyal companions and a war party that was steadfast uniting all the Arab clans under the black flag.

Does Islam fit with the 21ˢᵗ Century? Maybe you should ask it another way; did Islam make something out of the Dark Ages? Did a people with no hope in hell of being anything become something? In this modern day and age we cannot judge, we can only observe. Like a recon Marine deep in the jungles of Nam we observe through a scope at the canopies of history. And my next observation will show you a group of people a hundred thousand times more bloodthirsty than the early Muslims. If you think the Arabs were violent then pardon the following pages for what your mind is about to absorb. Without further ado, allow me to introduce you to the next warlike people in this chapter

The Mongols...

The Mongols were an Asian breed of warrior largely unknown to the outside world. Just like the Arabs of the Prophet's time, the Mongol clans were splintered tribes constantly killing one another. Yet despite alcoholism, mass rape and existential violence, the rolling hills of Mongolia birthed a people raised in freezing blizzards and draught seasons, food was scarce and was few and far in between for the clans to find. This led them to fight each other over territory. Mongolia was a no man's land, a barren vacuum in the vast expanse of the steppe. The only thing they had was perhaps the Silk Road and even that was cut off centuries prior. The steppe was a cluster of clans under different people like the Merkits, Tartars, Turks, Naimans and finally the Mongols. The one thing these people had going for them was their talent for war. They had been doing it for so long they knew nothing else. A long history of rulers, called Khans, had attempted to unite the unruly savages from the days of the Xiongnu to the Rouran Khaganate and all the way to the

Gokturk Khagnate. These kingdoms, or Khanates, ultimately failed in destroying sedentary civilizations like China which was the super power of that part of the world. It seemed these savage tribes would dissipate into a benign history without any significance to the world. That is until a boy was born in 1162 to the Mongols.

It is said the child was holding a blood clot in his clenched fist at the time of his birth. Was it an omen for things to come in his life? The father named the boy holding the ball of blood Temujin, which basically means Iron Devil. Temujin's father, Yesugei, who was the Khan of his tribe, was poisoned by the merkits when his son was still a boy, this led the tribe to pick up everything and abandon a 9 year old Temujin and his family. After being discarded by his own tribe and left to the wolves, Temujin sought to make a new ally as being a lone soul on the steppe almost meant certain death. He came into contact with a young boy called Jammuhka and together they swore an oath to become blood brothers. After a childhood of being captured, hunting, scavenging and living on alms, Temujin raised a small army at age 20. His blood brother Jammuhka became jealous and eventually the two detracted from each other....soon turning into bitter rivals then total enemies. Fighting between the clans of Jammuhka and Temujin came to an ultimatum when the two warlords faced each other in the battle of Thirteen Sides. Temujin was the victor and gave Jammukha a chance to join his army, yet his blood brother preferred to die, telling him in his last words –

'Just as there is only one sun in the sky there can only be one Khan'

In 1206 all the clans of Mongolia gathered for a Kuritai to announce Temujin as the supreme Khan of all the tribes under the eternal blue sky, his title became Genghis Khan....Universal Ruler. Genghis Khan would go on to conquer the greatest contiguous land empire in world history. The Mongols took more land in 25 years than the Romans did in 400. They shed more blood in one day than Khalid Bin Walid did in his entire career. Genghis Khans conquests were some of the bloodiest, ruthless and most genocidal expansions ever waged in Human existence. More people died under the Khans than all the deaths of World War 2 put together. One look at the size of the Mongol empire in 1279 and you'll start to get a picture of how widespread rape, murder and destruction had become on a global scale.

Basically....23, 500,000 km2 of the planet's surface was covered in blood stretching from Korea and Vietnam to Bagdad and Moscow. New research now suggests that the Mongol horde murdered so much human life that upwards of 700 million tonnes of carbon was absorbed from Earth's atmosphere. Meaning Genghis Khan reduced global warming by killing everything he came across. Not 10,000 tonnes, not 10 million tonnes.....700 million tonnes. That's according to Julia Pongratz at the Carnegie Institute of Global Ecology.

This is no joke....there are numerous horror stories like what they did in Merv, a golden metropolis hosting 700,000 people reduced to a festering mass grave in a few hours. The Iranian city of Nishapur with a million residents turned into a jungle of flesh and guts where mothers were impaled on large wooden stubs, not a single soul was spared. In fact when the Mongols left, they came back after a few days because they knew the survivors in the mountains were hiding and came back to see if their loved ones survived, a garrison of Mongol horsemen reappeared and massacred the last remnants too. These guys were a fucking nightmare. You think ISIS is bad? ISIS doesn't hold a quantum atom to the level of savagery of the Iron Devil. Temujin A.K.A 'Genghis Khan' and his sons like Ogadai, Chagatai and Mongy, his grandsons Ariq Boke and the legendary Kublai Khan obliterated the Chinese, the Persians, The Arabs, the Vietnamese, northern India and the Russians combined, then they fucked all their women. The Khans destroyed all their populations, their wealth, knowledge, history, art and institutions of learning. In the words of the Mongolian Godfather himself –

'I am the punishment of God...for if you had not committed great sins...God would not send a punishment like me upon you'

Temujin, the man who had ascended from near certain death and a harsh childhood to become the world's greatest warlord to ever walk the surface of the Earth suddenly died in 1227. The burial place of the great Khan remains unknown to this day. The funeral escorts that buried him were murdered so as nobody who was there could reveal the location to others. Then the murderers were themselves murdered for the same reason. One of the deadlier grandsons to continue the savage family business was Helagu; Helagu led the march on Baghdad, the capital of the Abbasids in 1258. The destruction that followed is the stuff of legend; the rivers of the Tigris ran with blood for days on end, the grand libraries were burned and a population of 2 million inhabitants was reduced to zilch. It is said that a Mongol woman could walk into a room of Muslim fanatics' naked holding a blade to slice their throats and they couldn't do a thing about it. That's like an American porn star walking into a room of Al Qaeda and bleeding each of them to death. It's hard to comprehend the level of fear these people exuded.

Very few films have been made on Genghis Khan, but if you were to watch a film about the man I suggest the following movie which is one my personal favourites. To get a glimpse of Temujin there is one film which portrays his ascent to power. That movie is 'Mongol' by Sergei Bordrov. It doesn't show his huge conquests of his later life, rather it shows a rising young warrior turned Khan turned Genghis Khan. 'Mongol'.....a totally epic movie and a solid trailer that stays true to historical authenticity of the people and time

There were not millions of these warriors, at any given time a Mongol army in its combined strength was no larger than 100,000.... more people go to Metallica concerts. So in retrospect whenever they took a city....every Mongol soldier would be assigned 24 people; kids, women, men, the old, 24 people for every soldier to carve up like lambs to the slaughter. Before their invasions, the population of China had roughly 250 million people. After they were done, the population was reduced to 60 million. Similar statistics can be said of Persia, Russia, central Asia and the Middle East. You couldn't do this with humanoid chain saws if you tried. The only other organisms on earth with as much tenacity to their killer mission are Bullet Ants.

The great expansions of the 7th century and the 13th century still affect our world to this day. Millions have died from the bloodletting and carnage that have taken place. Even Christian atrocities like the Spanish Inquisition and the discovery of the New World hold ranks as some of the more murderous stains on the world stage. God would never forgive us for what we've done to ourselves, think about all the people that have drowned, starved, been tortured and enslaved.... dragged across the Atlantic ocean in wooden ships or had their eyes plucked out of their heads. Baby girls buried before taking their first breath, young children diagnosed with cancer and AIDs. The world is a cold prison.

Even as recently as the 20th century 70 million Chinese were starved and left to perish in the cold snow because of their communist leader Mao Se Tung. Pol Pot murdered a million of his own people in 1975, leaving their bodies to melt in tropical killing fields. Soviet leader Josef Stalin liquidated all the lands and property of Russian hard working farmers, the Kulaks, and then murdered 10 million of them through starvation, forced marches, execution to the back of the head and purges. You know the story with Adolf Hitler and the Jews. The Japanese rape of Namkin, the Aztec slaughter of sacrificial virgins in the thousands, the Muslim conquest and rape of the Middle East, Genghis Khans floor cleaning of entire human populations, the suffering is endless, but not much longer...

According to cognitive psychologist Steven Pinker, we're living in an age of unparalleled plentifulness, prosperity and peaceful co operation between nations and religions. Tragedy and suffering have afflicted our history for as long as we've existed, but the 21st century is set to change that trend. Thanks to globalization effects such as multiculturalism, capitalism and the internet, worldwide communication has made it easier for people to converse with each other and spread our breakthroughs in science, medicine, robotic technology and even space travel. Think about that. We're becoming a unified global organism. Competition is slowly dying off.

For the first time it's possible to eradicate disease such as Small Pox. We've landed on the moon by harnessing the technology of Nazi scientists, our worst enemies ended up working on rocket travel and jet propulsion for the United States like Werner Von Braun. We can go to any country in a matter of hours, text and call anyone on the planet, share information in seconds on small television screens that fit in our palm. Put yourself in the shoes of a Christian Knight during the Middle Ages; you didn't have running water or a heat source inside your home. There was no electricity to power your oven, everything had to be gathered and collected outside. You had to cut up chunks of wood just to provide a means for warmth at night; the food you ate wasn't guaranteed to be on your table every morning because there were no super markets. You couldn't have a warm shower; you had to be friends with the paedophile church nobleman because he ensured the towns safety from invasion since he ran the local army. Everything was fucked up. No warmth, no heaters or electricity, no televisions or even sofa couches to sit on and watch the television. You're nothing but a lowly steed, you provide the best you can for your family and you eat hardened mutt and warm beef stew under the kettle. That was life....for hundreds of years. Life was rigid in Europe, in Mongolia, in Colonial America. Nobody got a free ride. So imagine his horror if that knight saw the world of today.

I mean, for fuck sake, we have holograms that project a person's ghost that can talk and interact with you, picture those 2,000 years ago. Where people can watch a video of someone on the other side of the planet and talk to them live, this shit is insane. At no point in history have we ever been this advanced, this prosperous, this healthy and so educated and intelligent. With a finance system so abundant that we pay slackers who don't work, we give them hand outs for their laziness to indulge in something called welfare. Millions are on this system where they receive a salary simply for doing nothing to earn that wage. That's how abundant and luxurious our society is. Which is why Genghis Khan did what he did to all those people, he left a quote to justify his wanton slaughter –

'Heaven grew weary of the excessive pride and luxury of China... I am from the Barbaric North. I wear the same clothing and eat the same food as the cowherds and horse-herders. We make the same sacrifices and we share our riches. I look upon the nation as a new-born child and I care for my soldiers as though they were my brothers'

He resented the Chinese for their luxurious wealth and plentifulness. Although it is a marvellous thing we are as advanced as we are, one must remember to not turn abundance into sloth and apathy. China had mountains of Gold, bronze palaces and weird traditions where women curled their feet for the ministers. The Mongols had bear fur huts, wolf skin uniforms and constant civil war and tribal in – fighting. It was destiny that someone had to be a great unifier of the clans. Even the Arabs of the prophet's time thought the same way. The excessive pride and luxury of the Byzantines and the Sassanids got on the nerves of Muhammad. His people were dying....they lived in the hottest desert on the planet, they had to survive while cleaning blood from their robes after every battle...and these dudes up north are living in big monasteries and eating like kings? He wasn't going to let those Greco-Anatolian fags get away with their sissy attitude. Those churchy white cottoned monks and the golden staffs they carried around, the grape eating haughty kings and their nobility that lived off the wealth of the commoner.

The Arabs were not commoners....they were the baddest motherfuckers with sword and belief. Muhammad knew this, he done a magic trick, he made the Arab tribes unite together then use their abilities to win wars against those silky soft cocks in Turkey and Iran. Them pussies had it coming. If you're an Arab reading this, especially if you're Sunni....never be ashamed of what you are. Your forefathers like Khalid Bin Walid were hardcore sword carrying lions of Tuhweed. No regret for what Islam did in the 7th century. Like the bearded king Leonidas from the movie 300....'NO MERCY!'

There is lots of regret for those enlightened haughty civilizations for being so effeminate and meek, people with too much softness deserve a good blooding....Islam was the masculine punishment to their humanity. Umar and his men were fierce zealots because they fought with tenacity and brutality. So imagine if an unstoppable force met an immovable object and the Martyrs ran into the Mongols. The Muslim Arabs were raised in the heat of the desert; the Mongols were raised in the freezing blizzards of the Tundra. Which weather system produces tougher people...extreme heat or extreme cold? Both their leaders never lost any battles...I got mad respect for Khaled and Genghis Khan.

CHAPTER 5

Social Horror Story

So what's the reason for writing this book? Is it to describe history? What's Genghis Khan or Khalid Bin Walid got to do with the second millennium of the modern world? Well I'll spell it out for you....America is the modern fighting culture. The only world power which mass produces a masculine war like people. And the reason I wrote this memoir...is because I see America slowly losing that edge. As simple as that. The world's greatest super power is turning into a meek. Not because of its military. No, what makes it weak is its recent trendy pop culture.

It now glorifies sissy and excessive behaviour in its rap stars and a total worship of childish immaturity in music videos, these conditions are right to shape the people into acting and behaving a certain way. The culture has been emasculated...just like those Persians or Byzantines before somebody from a very hot place decided to beat them to a bloody pulp. Soft elopement behaviour is never an excuse....not for the Mongols, not for the Shaheeds and not for bloodthirsty America. What I'm saying is America went from Tupac and the first Marshal Mathers LP album replete with rape, throat slitting and violence to comb overs, skinny jeans and a neutered sense of happiness through social media. You lost your balls.

America's cultural dominance was delivered through a medium in the early 20th century called Hollywood, Hollywood became a global titan of influence wherein its motion pictures sprouted up everywhere in the world, even in the Soviet Union, which means America could influence the minds of people anywhere it wanted to. The Ten Commandments was huge, so was Gone with the Wind and the Wizard of Oz. This cultural dominance planted the seeds for an even bigger take over.....with violence, blood and guts. Modern American movie culture is violent, doesn't matter if it's Pulp Fiction, Kill Bill or Scream. The reason I wrote this book is because I see that culture fading away...and I want it back

But like the saying goes

'Don't be sad it's passed, just be happy that it happened'

and that's ok, I would have been fine with that just perfect. I wouldn't need to write about people's favourite music and nostalgia if one thing...if America didn't move away from bloodshed on its screens and masculinity in its men. Not for weakness to take its place. Because wether we want to accept it or not America leads the world. Wherever the red, white and blue goes the others follow. France, Russia, Germany, China, Italy, Thailand, Brazil they all follow US trends.

All those European countries, all those Asian countries, the South and Latin Americans, their people are soft and affectionate. That's why their accents are charming...but that's because their people are weak and their voices show it. The reasons America is hated by the world are the same reasons that make it strong as a nation; aggressive arrogance, obnoxious assertiveness, fearless dominance, an ass kicking attitude and a total grip on being a fucking badass. The world isn't jealous, it can't believe a country such as America has something they completely lack...a hardcore psyche. America's empire even reaches onto the moon. They're not afraid to be like Leonidas, they are the 300 of the world. That's why America rules and you don't. Just like the arrows blocking the sky, America took warheads from the British, the Germans and the Japanese and smashed them off with a spear. It's a culture not concerned with folklore or traditions, not festivals or tales and myths. All that garbage is bullshit. Hansel and Gretel, Homers Illiad, Snow white and the 7 dwarves, you take any cultural tale of the world and I bet you it's got nothing on the lobby shootout scene from the Matrix –

'Not by the hair on your chinny chin chin'

OR

'Would you please remove any metallic items you are carrying; keys, loose change'

The rest of the world would be like that dude calling for back up, and we all know what happened to him in the lobby. America rules the globe like no other nation in the history of earth. But her true dominance lies in her soft power. The Internet, Microsoft, Play Station, Hollywood; there isn't a kid in the world that doesn't know what Coca Cola is. Everybody has seen the McDonalds sign. Its movie industry floods audiences' eyes day and night; its music infects teenager's souls with filth and gutter talk about murder and violence. The United States is a degenerate culture; not in the form of Sodom and Gomorrah, more in the form of Genghis Khan's Mongolia. A country where mass killings are so widespread it's become the culture of its music and movies everywhere, not 'a' culture, THE culture. All their best rappers illustrated murder and violence, every single one of them. Tupac, perhaps the premier rapper of all time, made Hit em up. You think of romantic European folk songs and compare them to Hit em Up.

'And Mumma bear said whose being sleeping in my bed'

Then

'First of fuck your bitch the and click you claim, west side when we ride come equipped we game'

Hip Hop is a reflection of the violence and animosity in urban America. Then you have Eminem with Kill You, the greatest white rapper was furthering the bloodshed in Kim or Go to Sleep. This isn't a fanciful dream; these are people reflecting the conditions of their society. America was murderously steeped in depravity. And that's why I love the culture, it was a country founded on genocide, slavery and revolution. That animosity has kept with its mindset. It burns the fat off their souls and keeps them hateful and bitter. They're in a perpetual self cannibalizing murder illusion.

US soldiers don't need to invade your country with an army to shape how you see the world....they shape your mind every day with music and movies. Think of 28 Weeks Later, Final Destination or The Hateful 8. All this stuff affects how people are conditioned... when you grow a tolerance to violence you become accustomed to desensitization. When you're desensitized you turn out like the characters you watch. Let me ask you something, what's the most violent movie you've ever watched? Let me guess it's a Hollywood movie? Let's do a demonstration....if you don't think Hollywood is not the most violent thing on earth, hop on your computer or phone, go to You Tube and watch the final battle in Rambo 4

Rambo 4 final battle......your babies are watching this, mums and dads so it's no game

That's why I wrote this, I want that culture to remain firmly in place. It worships psychopathy. It hardens the soul of a young child and makes for a Spartan-like population. I don't want to see the world's greatest power become an effeminate like Brazil or France. You can judge a population's fighting tenacity by the way they speak. The French sound like cotton buds. You think the Swedes sound manly and masculine with their tone of voice? When was the last time Switzerland fought a war?

The Americans are mostly of European stock but make no mistake, they hail from a warrior breed, so do the Latinos and black people. They're all descendent of warrior tribes regardless of race, be it Germanic and Scottish highlanders, Zulu tiger archers or Aztec heart ripping psycho motherfuckers. They don't come from soft bloodlines. Doesn't matter if you're white, black, Latino, mixed, Asian, southerner, northerner or even Chicarilla native Indian....the country these people inhabit has evoked a warrior. I'm not talking about your average middle class family from Ohio, I don't mean those chicken shit characters from Modern Family, they're not real Americans.

So really what's the problem? I'll tell you the problem right now. Ever since the election of Obama, American culture has slowly turned from that masculinity and gone piss weak and soft. That's putting it lightly. Their music has changed from violence and animosity into 'Star ships were meant to Fly' and 'All about the Bass'. Its entertainment now revels with immaturity. That's just music. What annoys me is the fashion; a hipster fashion called swag where young men are neutered and emasculated by the trend of skinny chinos, fitted tops and snap back caps. It's not just in some cities, it's everywhere in the world. Young teenage men thinking it's cool that their tight little fancy pants are avant garde, their snap backs are urban and their tight shirts are somehow new age.

You're all a bunch of fucking pussies, you hear me reader? I mean let's be honest for a second here....does that description fit with a bro sporting an Adidas cap, a goatee and 200 CCs of testosterone? I guess it's ok if you're over 40 and your past the juvenile stage of life, but young men, especially under the age of 25 should be rocking bulky trousers and sporting over sized tees like it was the 90s on crack. Why? Because its fucking attitude that's why. I wanna see attitude in the youngsters, not chinos and comb overs. What are you, a law abiding do gooder citizen or a goddamn rebel without a cause who listen to Limp Bizkit and pisses on Ed Sheeran CDs? My sort of bros and bad bitches I'm describing were alive and flourishing in the 90s. Where did they go?

I don't want to sound like the old man that complains about the new generation but the world I'm living in for the last 8 years has been a nightmare. To sum it up, the 2010s have been the worst decade of the modern world to date. Not because of world wars of mass starvations but because of emasculation. America was the last hope for the world because of the pages I previously discussed about its cruelty. Now it's turned into a joke. Like Temujin someone has to wake everyone up to this shit. I couldn't take it anymore; my blood boiled to such a point years ago that there was nowhere to go, nowhere to run or find escapism; I was trapped in this matrix of bubbly childish music videos and stupidity, senseless viral social media sensations where people acted without common sense. And this twitter culture was pushing that mentality; it was conditioning people of all ages to be gluttonous, stupid and mindless. One song that promotes this mindless nonsense is the dub step song Turn down for what.

You watch that pile of horse shit and witness the grotesque stupidity of people; it's a reflection of the last decade we've been living in. Case in point, we're a fucking joke! Our culture is a joke, America has gone from something to be feared and respected to a laughing stock. It was once a fearless Titan, now it has fat people dancing in silky colours like 'All about the Bass'. Do you get my point? Adults are behaving like children, children are growing up in this colourful nightmare, everything is pink and rosy and the skies weep unicorns and the trees sing with wub wub sounds. Do you see where I'm coming from? We've lost our seriousness, we've lost our intensity. We've let silly people sit on the throne where the fearsome lion truly belongs. Fuck All about the Bass.....Star ships were not meant to fly through the radio waves. If you don't believe me about immaturity, watch those two videos and discover how childish and nonsensical people with power have become. That's the 2010s.

Because somebody has to wake up to this immature and superficial garbage, nobody did, not for a long time. I searched internet chat rooms to find if other people realized the gravity of the situation, of what we're in, I went onto You Tube comment sections, I made posts on Facebook, I even talked to people on the street. Everyone was oblivious. Because surprise surprise they were too busy being absorbed on their smart phone, another fucking trap, so it's like a trap inside a trap inside a prison inside the Matrix. They were too busy snap chatting and instagraming and facebooking, they were on twitter, while the world burns in pink flavours and fake wub wub sounds. We're living a modern day fucking horror....and I bet you were so sucked into the Matrix you didn't even care or realize. Am I right? What started all this?

There was a video that started this global trend of immaturity. It enabled clowns and dumb asses to become well paid jesters. The first video in You Tube history to reach a billion views...Gangnam Style. Talk about an idiotic, talentless, moronic fucking hack. There are no words in the entire Universe that hosts sentient life which could describe my hatred for Gangnam Style. I hate it with more passion that Hitlers hatred of all the Jews on planet Earth. It is more sickening to my eyes than a thousand onions in the heat. There are no levels in Hell I wouldn't go to and destroy that thing. The greatest calamity in Earths existence wasn't the K2 extinction event...it was the widespread conditioning of Gangnam Style.

When that thing went global, when its tentacles of stupidity and complete lack of common sense entered the living rooms of every street I made an oath with God. In my heart of hearts I vouched with sheer belief that I would bring my vengeance against this disorder of music, I would desecrate its idol worship and bring down this golden cow that a billion people were dancing around. People should not be happy, they should be serious. Like the ancient proverb goes –

'Happy people don't make history'

Muhammad was never happy with his people; Genghis Khan was greatly resentful of China's softness and arrogance. Adolf Hitler was a vengeance set by God to bring world destruction. The Lord himself really did bring the globe to an apocalypse in 2012 when Gangnam Style came out, America experienced the greatest hurricane in its history and the Middle East exploded from Tunisia to Egypt and Bahrain. So all you happy people, smiling and snapchatting and posting a viral video...your judgement day is coming motherfucker. It's not right that a Korean song filled with immaturity such as Gangnam Style takes centre stage and promotes global dumbassery. It's not right, ever.

The Koreans as a people were conquered and enslaved by the Mongols then the Japanese, two of Asia's fiercest warrior races.

Koreans are a fucking pussy breed and they should stay in their place. They were no match for Kublai Khan or the Bushido code and they shouldn't challenge the land of Tupac and Rage against the Machine. Like the song says I had to Wake Up...I had to Rage against the Machine so I wrote a book dedicated to a time opposite of today. I didn't talk into a pay phone to get my message across to you....I'm doing it the old way, with words on paper. And I hope you wake up and realize this message. I don't like this world we're living in. America became a circus in the 2010s. Your millennial teens are spoiled half assed qeafs that should be conscripted into the French Foreign Legion. Deprive them of food, water and Facebook. If Americans at a young age were raised like the intro to 300 then there would be no cop outs like the democrats or the radical left. You wouldn't get wimpy little men with pink hair demanding gender neutral rights and other shit, they would be smacked fucking silly and made to harden or perish. You got me? Harden or perish!

Remember that young Spartan boy punching the blood out of his opponents mouth in 300, you remember him standing under the clouds with a swelled black eye and a nasty fucking stare. The Agoge is what makes Marines and Special Forces. That's the material the Spartans were made of at heart, it's what the Romans were made of, it's what Muhammads armies were made of and it's what flowed in the blood of Temujin and his wolf skin warriors. That's why it's up to America to cut this immature and artificial shit out. The 2000s as a decade promoted north American warrior tenacity; 300 was made in that period, so was the Bourne trilogy, Eminem and the Iraq war. The 21st century doesn't belong to the childish or the senseless.... we should not be remembered with horse dancing gestures. The Americans rule the world; but now you've been softened, buttered up and turned weak. Come back as the fearless lions you motherfuckers truly are, I wrote this book to restore American cultural edge

Like 300....Return a King and the world will bow
'NO PRISONERS, NO MERCY!!'

'All I fear we have done is awaken a sleeping giant filled with a terrible resolve'

— Admiral Yamamoto after the attack on Pearl Harbour, United States

Printed in the United States
By Bookmasters